MICROWAVE RECIPES FOR BEGINNERS

MANY DELICIOUS AND BUSY RECIPES FOR BUSY PEOPLE

JEREMY LENNON

Table of Contents

Minted Aubergine Dip 13
Aubergine Dip with Tomatoes and Mixed Herbs........................... 14
Middle Eastern Aubergine and Tahini Dip..................................... 15
Turkish Aubergine Dip... 16
Greek Aubergine Dip 17
Bagna Cauda 18
Aubergine Casserole.. 19
Pickled Cocktail Mushrooms 21
Stuffed Baked Aubergines with Eggs and Pine Nuts...................... 22
Greek Mushrooms.. 23
Artichokes Vinaigrette 24
Caesar Salad... 25
Dutch Chicory with Egg and Butter 26
Egg Mayonnaise 27
Eggs with Skordalia Mayonnaise 28
Scotch Woodcock... 29
Eggs with Swedish Mayonnaise... 30
Turkish Bean Salad... 31
Bean Salad with Egg... 32
Potted Kipper 33
Potted Shrimp 34
Baked Stuffed Egg Avocados 35

Tomato and Cheese-stuffed Avocados	36
Scandinavian Rollmop and Apple Salad	37
Rollmop and Apple Salad with Curry Sauce	38
Leafy Salad with Goat's Cheese and Warm Dressing	39
Jellied Tomato Sundaes	40
Stuffed Tomatoes	41
Italian Stuffed Tomatoes	42
Tomato and Chicken Salad Cups	43
Chopped Egg and Onion	44
Quiche Lorraine	45
Cheese and Tomato Quiche	47
Smoked Salmon Quiche	47
Prawn Quiche	47
Spinach Quiche	47
Mediterranean Quiche	48
Asparagus Quiche	49
Devilled Walnuts	50
Curried Brazil Nuts	51
Blue Cheese and Pecan Flan	52
Rich Liver Pâté	54
Hot and Sour Crab Soup	55
Easy Oriental Soup	57
Liver Dumpling Soup	58
Cream of Carrot Soup	59
Chilled Carrot and Leek Soup	60
Carrot and Coriander Soup	61
Carrot with Orange Soup	61

Lettuce Cream Soup 62
Green Purée Soup 63
Parsnip and Parsley Soup with Wasabi 64
Sweet Potato Soup 64
Cream of Vegetable Soup 65
Green Pea Soup 66
Squash Soup 66
Cream of Mushroom Soup 66
Cream of Pumpkin Soup 67
Cock-a-leekie Soup 68
Scotch Broth 69
Israeli Chicken and Avocado Soup 70
Avocado Soup with Beetroot 70
Bortsch 71
Cold Bortsch 72
Creamy Cold Bortsch 72
Orange Lentil Soup 73
Orange Lentil Soup with Cheese and Toasted Cashews 74
Lentil Soup with Tomato Garnish 74
Yellow Pea Soup 75
French Onion Soup 76
Minestrone 77
Minestrone Genovese 78
Italian Potato Soup 79
Fresh Tomato and Celery Soup 80
Tomato Soup with Avocado Dressing 81
Chilled Cheese and Onion Soup 82

Swiss-style Cheese Soup 83
Avgolemono Soup 84
Cream of Cucumber Soup with Pastis 85
Curry Soup with Rice 86
Vichyssoise 87
Chilled Cucumber Soup with Yoghurt 88
Chilled Spinach Soup with Yoghurt 89
Sherried Chilled Tomato Soup 90
New England Fish Chowder 91
Crab Soup 92
Crab and Lemon Soup 93
Lobster Bisque 93
Dried Packet Soup 93
Canned Condensed Soup 94
Reheating Soups 94
Warming Eggs for Cooking 94
Poached Eggs 95
Fried (Sautéed) Eggs 96
Piperade 97
Piperade with Gammon 98
Piperada 98
Eggs Florentine 99
Poached Egg Rossini 100
Aubergine Egg Scramble 100
Classic Omelette 102
Flavoured Omelettes 103
Brunch Omelette 104

Poached Egg with Melted Cheese *105*

Eggs Benedict *105*

Omelette Arnold Bennett *106*

Tortilla *107*

Spanish Omelette with Mixed Vegetables *108*

Spanish Omelette with Ham *109*

Cheesy Eggs in Celery Sauce *109*

Eggs Fu Yung *110*

Pizza Omelette *111*

Soufflé Omelette *112*

Lemon Soufflé Omelette *112*

Orange Soufflé Omelette *113*

Almond and Apricot Soufflé Omelette *113*

Raspberry Soufflé Omelette *113*

Strawberry Soufflé Omelette *114*

Soufflé Omelette with Toppings *114*

Baked Egg with Cream *114*

Baked Egg Neapolitan *115*

Cheese Fondue *116*

Fondue with Cider *117*

Fondue with Apple Juice *117*

Pink Fondue *117*

Smoky Fondue *118*

German Beer Fondue *118*

Fondue with Fire *118*

Curried Fondue *118*

Fonduta *119*

Mock Cheese and Tomato Fondue 119
Cheese Fondue 120
Fondue with Cider 121
Fondue with Apple Juice 121
Pink Fondue 121
Smoky Fondue 122
German Beer Fondue 122
Fondue with Fire 122
Curried Fondue 122
Fonduta 123
Mock Cheese and Tomato Fondue 123
Mock Cheese and Celery Fondue 124
Italian Cheese, Cream and Egg Fondue 125
Dutch Farmhouse Fondue 126
Farmhouse Fondue with a Kick 127
Baked Egg Flamenco Style 128
Bread and Butter Cheese and Parsley Pudding 129
   Bread and Butter Cheese and Parsley Pudding with Cashew Nuts
.... 130
Four-cheese Bread and Butter Pudding 130
Cheese and Egg Crumpets 131
Upside-down Cheese and Tomato Pudding 132
Pizza Crumpets 133
Gingered Sea Bass with Onions 134
Trout Packets 135
Shining Monkfish with Slender Beans 136
Shining Prawns with Mangetout 137

Normandy Cod with Cider and Calvados *138*
Fish Paella *140*
Soused Herrings *142*
Moules Marinières *143*
Mackerel with Rhubarb and Raisin Sauce *145*
Herring with Apple Cider Sauce *146*
Carp in Jellied Sauce *147*
Rollmops with Apricots *148*
Poached Kipper *149*
Prawns Madras *150*
Martini Plaice Rolls with Sauce *151*
Shellfish Ragout with Walnuts *153*
Cod Hot-pot *155*
Smoked Cod Hot-pot *156*
Monkfish in Golden Lemon Cream Sauce *156*
Sole in Golden Lemon Cream Sauce *158*
Salmon Hollandaise *158*
Salmon Hollandaise with Coriander *159*
Salmon Mayonnaise Flake *160*
Mediterranean-style Salmon Roast *161*
Kedgeree with Curry *162*
Kedgeree with Smoked Salmon *163*
Smoked Fish Quiche *164*
Louisiana Prawn Gumbo *165*
Monkfish Gumbo *166*
Mixed Fish Gumbo *166*
Trout with Almonds *167*

Prawns Provençale *168*
Plaice in Celery Sauce with Toasted Almonds *169*
Fillets in Tomato Sauce with Marjoram *170*
Fillets in Mushroom Sauce with Watercress *170*
Hashed Cod with Poached Eggs *171*
Haddock and Vegetables in Cider Sauce *173*
Seaside Pie *174*
Smoky Fish Toppers *176*
Coley Fillets with Leek and Lemon Marmalade *177*
Seafish in a Jacket *178*
Swedish Cod with Melted Butter and Egg *179*
Seafood Stroganoff *180*
Fresh Tuna Stroganoff *181*
White Fish Ragout Supreme *181*
Salmon Mousse *183*
Dieters' Salmon Mousse *185*
Crab Mornay *185*
Tuna Mornay *186*
Red Salmon Mornay *186*
Seafood and Walnut Combo *187*
Salmon Ring with Dill *189*
Mixed Fish Ring with Parsley *190*
Cod Casserole with Bacon and Tomatoes *191*
Slimmers' Fish Pot *192*
Roast Chicken *194*
Glazed Roast Chicken *195*
Tex-Mex Chicken *196*

Coronation Chicken *197*
Chicken Veronique *198*
Chicken in Vinegar Sauce with Tarragon *199*
Danish Roast Chicken with Parsley Stuffing *200*
Chicken Simla *200*
Spicy Chicken with Coconut and Coriander *201*
Spicy Rabbit *202*
Spicy Turkey *202*
Chicken Bredie with Tomatoes *203*
Chinese Red Cooked Chicken *204*
Aristocratic Chicken Wings *205*
Chicken Chow Mein *206*
Chicken Chop Suey *207*
Express Marinaded Chinese Chicken *207*
Hong Kong Chicken with Mixed Vegetables and Bean Sprouts ... *208*
Chicken with Golden Dragon Sauce *209*
Ginger Chicken Wings with Lettuce *210*
Bangkok Coconut Chicken *211*
Chicken Satay *212*
Peanut Chicken *213*
Indian Chicken with Yoghurt *214*
Japanese Chicken with Eggs *215*
Portuguese Chicken Casserole *216*
English-style Spicy Chicken Casserole *217*
Compromise Tandoori Chicken *217*

Minted Aubergine Dip

Serves 6–8

750 g/1½ lb aubergines (eggplants)
Juice of 1 lemon
20 ml/4 tsp olive oil
1–2 garlic cloves, crushed
250 ml/8 fl oz/1 cup fromage frais or quark
15 ml/1 tbsp chopped mint leaves
1.5 ml/¼ tsp caster (superfine) sugar
7.5–10 ml/1½–2 tsp salt

Top and tail the aubergines and halve them lengthways. Arrange them on a large plate, cut sides down, and cover with kitchen paper. Cook on Full for 8–9 minutes or until soft. Scoop the flesh out of the skins directly into a food processor and add the remaining ingredients. Process to a smooth and creamy purée. Spoon into a serving bowl, cover and chill lightly before serving.

Aubergine Dip with Tomatoes and Mixed Herbs

Serves 6–8

750 g/1½ lb aubergines (eggplants)
5 ml/1 tsp chopped mint leaves
75 ml/3 tsp chopped coriander (cilantro) leaves
5 ml/1 tsp chopped parsley
3 tomatoes, blanched, skinned, seeded and finely chopped

Top and tail the aubergines and halve them lengthways. Arrange them on a large plate, cut sides down, and cover with kitchen paper. Cook on Full for 8–9 minutes or until soft. Scoop the flesh out of the skins directly into a food processor and add the remaining ingredients except the tomatoes. Process to a smooth and creamy purée. Stir in the tomatoes, then spoon into a serving bowl, cover and chill lightly before serving.

Middle Eastern Aubergine and Tahini Dip

Serves 6–8

750 g/1½ lb aubergines (eggplants)
45 ml/3 tbsp tahini (sesame seed paste)
Juice of 1 small lemon
1 garlic clove, thinly sliced
25 ml/1½ tbsp olive oil
1 small onion, sliced
60 ml/4 tbsp coarsely chopped coriander (cilantro) leaves
5 ml/1 tsp caster (superfine) sugar
5–10 ml/1–2 tsp salt

Top and tail the aubergines and halve them lengthways. Arrange them on a large plate, cut sides down, and cover with kitchen paper. Cook on Full for 8–9 minutes or until soft. Scoop the flesh out of the skins directly into a food processor. Add the remaining ingredients and salt to taste. Process to a smooth and creamy purée. Spoon into a serving bowl and serve at room temperature.

Turkish Aubergine Dip

Serves 6–8

750 g/1½ lb aubergines (eggplants)
30 ml/2 tbsp olive oil
Juice of 1 large lemon
2.5–5 ml/½–1 tsp salt
2.5 ml/½ tsp caster (superfine) sugar
Black olives, red (bell) pepper strips and tomato wedges, to garnish

Top and tail the aubergines and halve them lengthways. Arrange them on a large plate, cut sides down, and cover with kitchen paper. Cook on Full for 8–9 minutes or until soft. Scoop the flesh out of the skins directly into a food processor and add the remaining ingredients. Process to a semi-smooth purée. Pile into a serving dish and garnish with olives, red pepper and tomato wedges.

Greek Aubergine Dip

Serves 6–8

750 g/1½ lb aubergines (eggplants)
1 small onion, coarsely grated
2 garlic cloves, thinly sliced
5 ml/1 tsp malt vinegar
5 ml/1 tsp lemon juice
150 ml/¼ pt/2/3 cup mild olive oil
2 large tomatoes, blanched, seeded and coarsely chopped
Parsley, green or red (bell) pepper rings and small black olives, to garnish

Top and tail the aubergines and halve them lengthways. Arrange them on a large plate, cut sides down, and cover with kitchen paper. Cook on Full for 8–9 minutes or until soft. Scoop the flesh out of the skins directly into a food processor and add the onion, garlic, vinegar, lemon juice and oil. Process to a smooth purée. Spoon into a large bowl and mix in the tomatoes. Pile into a serving dish and garnish with parsley, pepper rings and olives.

Bagna Cauda

Serves 4–6

An immensely rich and unique anchovy dip from Italy which, once made, should be kept warm over a spirit stove on the dining table. The dunks are generally raw or cooked vegetables. Use only mild and delicate pale gold extra virgin olive oil, otherwise the flavour may be too strong.

30 ml/2 tbsp olive oil
25 g/1 oz/2 tbsp unsalted (sweet) butter
1 garlic clove, crushed
50 g/2 oz/1 small can anchovy fillets in oil
60 ml/4 tbsp finely chopped parsley
15 ml/1 tbsp finely chopped basil leaves

Put the oil, butter and garlic into a non-metallic flameproof bowl. Add the oil from the can of anchovies, the parsley and basil. Finely chop the anchovies and add to the bowl. Part-cover the bowl with a plate and cook on Defrost for 3–4 minutes until the dip is just warmed. Transfer to a lit spirit stove and keep warm while eating.

Aubergine Casserole

Serves 4

A Louisiana recipe, which returned with me from this steamy part of North America.

2 aubergines (eggplants), about 550 g/1¼ lb in all
1 celery stalk, finely chopped
1 large onion, finely chopped
½ green (bell) pepper, seeded and finely chopped
30 ml/2 tbsp sunflower or corn oil
3 tomatoes, skinned and chopped
75 g/3 oz/1½ cups fresh white breadcrumbs
Salt and freshly ground black pepper
50 g/2 oz/½ cup Cheddar cheese, grated

Using a sharp knife, score the skin of each aubergine lengthways all the way round. Place on a plate, cover with kitchen paper and cook on Full for 6 minutes, turning once. They should feel tender but, if not, cook for a further 1–2 minutes. Halve each along the scoring, then scoop the pulp into blender or food processor and discard the skins. Process to a purée. Put the celery, onion, green pepper and oil into a 2 litre/3½ pt/8½ cup casserole dish (Dutch oven), cover with a plate and cook on Full for 3 minutes. Mix in the aubergine purée, tomatoes, breadcrumbs and salt and pepper to taste and cook on Full for a further 3 minutes. Uncover, sprinkle with the cheese and reheat, uncovered, on Full for 2 minutes. Allow to stand for 2 minutes before serving.

Pickled Cocktail Mushrooms

Serves 8

60 ml/4 tbsp red wine vinegar
60 ml/4 tbsp sunflower or corn oil
1 onion, very thinly sliced
5 ml/1 tsp salt
15 ml/1 tbsp chopped coriander (cilantro) leaves
5 ml/1 tsp mild made mustard
15 ml/1 tbsp light soft brown sugar
5 ml/1 tsp Worcestershire sauce
Cayenne pepper
350 g/12 oz button mushrooms

Put the vinegar, oil, onion, salt, coriander, mustard, sugar and Worcestershire sauce into a 2 litre/ 3½ pt/8½ cup casserole dish (Dutch oven) with a sprinkling of cayenne pepper. Cover with a plate and heat on Full for 6 minutes. Stir in the mushrooms. When cold, cover and chill for about 12 hours. Drain and serve with a creamy dip.

Stuffed Baked Aubergines with Eggs and Pine Nuts

Serves 2

2 aubergines (eggplants), about 550 g/1¼ lb in all

10 ml/2 tsp lemon juice

75 g/3 oz/1½ cups fresh white or brown breadcrumbs

45 ml/3 tbsp toasted pine nuts

7.5 ml/1½ tsp salt

1 garlic clove, crushed

3 hard-boiled (hard-cooked) eggs, chopped

60 ml/4 tbsp milk

5 ml/1 tsp dried mixed herbs

20 ml/4 tsp olive oil

Using a sharp knife, score the skin of each aubergine lengthways all the way round. Place on a plate, cover with kitchen paper and cook on Full for 6 minutes, turning once. They should feel tender but, if not, cook for a further 1–2 minutes. Halve each along the scoring, then scoop the pulp into a blender or food processor, leaving the skins intact. Add the lemon juice and process to a smooth purée. Scrape into a bowl and mix in all the remaining ingredients except the oil. Spoon into the aubergine skins, then arrange on a plate with the narrow ends towards the centre. Trickle the oil over the top, cover with kitchen paper and reheat on Full for 4 minutes. Eat hot or cold.

Greek Mushrooms

Serves 4

1 bouquet garni sachet
1 garlic clove, crushed
2 bay leaves
60 ml/4 tbsp water
30 ml/2 tbsp lemon juice
15 ml/1 tbsp wine vinegar
15 ml/1 tbsp olive oil
5 ml/1 tsp salt
450 g/1 lb button mushrooms
30 ml/2 tbsp chopped parsley

Put all the ingredients except the mushrooms and parsley into a large bowl. Cover with a plate and heat on Full for 4 minutes. Stir in the mushrooms, cover as before and cook on Full for a further 3½ minutes. Cool, cover, then chill for several hours. Remove the bouquet garni then, using a draining spoon, lift the mushrooms on to four plates, sprinkle each with the parsley and serve.

Artichokes Vinaigrette

Serves 4

450g/1lb Jerusalem artichokes
Vinaigrette dressing, home-made or bought
10 ml/2 tsp chopped parsley
5 ml/1 tsp chopped tarragon

Put the artichokes and a little water into a dish and cover with a plate. Cook on Full for 10 minutes, turning the dish twice. Drain thoroughly and slice thickly. Coat with the vinaigrette dressing while still warm. Divide between four plates and sprinkle with the parsley and tarragon.

Caesar Salad

Serves 4

A unique salad, created in the twenties by Caesar Cardini, which unusually features coddled eggs. It's a superbly simple starter yet has classic chic.

1 cos (romaine) lettuce, chilled
1 garlic clove, crushed
60 ml/4 tbsp extra virgin olive oil
Salt and freshly ground black pepper
2 large eggs
5 ml/1 tsp Worcestershire sauce
Juice of 2 lemons, strained
90 ml/6 tbsp freshly grated Parmesan cheese
50 g/2 oz/1 cup garlic croûtons

Cut the lettuce across into 5 cm/2 in pieces and place in a salad bowl with the garlic, oil and seasoning to taste. Toss gently. To coddle the eggs, line a cereal bowl with clingfilm (plastic wrap) and break in the eggs. Cook, uncovered, on Defrost for 1½ minutes. Add to the salad bowl with all the remaining ingredients and toss again until thoroughly mixed. Arrange on dinner plates and serve straight away.

Dutch Chicory with Egg and Butter

Serves 4

8 heads chicory (Belgian endive)
30 ml/2 tbsp lemon juice
75 ml/5 tbsp boiling water
5 ml/1 tsp salt
75 g/3 oz/1/3 cup butter, at kitchen temperature and quite soft
4 hard-boiled (hard-cooked) eggs, chopped

Trim the chicory and cut out a cone-shaped piece from the base of each to prevent a bitter taste. Arrange the chicory in a single layer in a 20 cm/8 in diameter dish and add the lemon juice and water. Sprinkle with the salt. Cover with clingfilm (plastic wrap) and slit it twice to allow the steam to escape. Cook on Full for 15 minutes. Allow to stand 3 minutes, then drain. While the chicory is cooking, beat the butter until light and creamy. Mix in the eggs. Arrange the chicory on four warmed plates and top with the egg mixture. Eat straight away.

Egg Mayonnaise

Serves 1

One of France's standard starters, Egg Mayonnaise is reliably appetising and can be varied according to taste.

Shredded lettuce leaves
1–2 hard-boiled (hard-cooked) eggs, halved
Mayonnaise Sauce, or use bought mayonnaise
4 canned anchovy fillets in oil
1 tomato, cut into wedges

Arrange the lettuce on a plate. Top with the eggs, cut sides down. Coat fairly thickly with the mayonnaise, then garnish to taste with the anchovies and tomato wedges.

Eggs with Skordalia Mayonnaise

Serves 4

A simplified version of a complex garlic and breadcrumb mayonnaise sauce that complements the full flavour and texture of the eggs.

150 ml/¼ pt/2/3 cup Mayonnaise Sauce
1 garlic clove, crushed
10 ml/2 tsp fresh white breadcrumbs
15 ml/1 tbsp ground almonds
10 ml/2 tsp lemon juice
10 ml/2 tsp chopped parsley
Shredded lettuce leaves
2 or 4 hard-boiled (hard-cooked) eggs, halved
1 red onion, very thinly sliced
Small Greek black olives, to garnish

Mix together the mayonnaise, garlic, breadcrumbs, almonds, lemon juice and parsley. Arrange the lettuce on a plate, then top with the egg halves. Coat with the mayonnaise mixture, then garnish with the onion slices and olives.

Scotch Woodcock

Serves 4

This belongs to the old league of City gentlemen's clubs and, served hot, remains one of the most up-market of canapés.

4 slices bread
Butter
Gentleman's Relish or anchovy paste
2 quantities Extra Creamy Scrambled Eggs
A few canned anchovy fillets in oil, to garnish

Toast the bread, then spread with butter. Spread thinly with Gentleman's Relish or anchovy paste, cut each slice into quarters and keep warm. Make the Extra Creamy Scrambled Eggs and spoon on to the toast quarters. Garnish with anchovy fillets.

Eggs with Swedish Mayonnaise

Serves 4

Shredded lettuce leaves
1–2 hard-boiled (hard-cooked) eggs, halved
25 ml/1½ tbsp apple purée (apple sauce)
Caster (superfine) sugar
150 ml/¼ pt/2/3 cup Mayonnaise Sauce, or use bought mayonnaise
5 ml/1 tsp horseradish sauce
5–10 ml/1–2 tsp black or orange mock caviare
1 red-skinned eating (dessert) apple, thinly sliced

Arrange the lettuce on a plate. Top with the eggs, cut sides down. Sweeten the apple purée lightly with caster sugar, then mix into the mayonnaise with the horseradish sauce. Coat the eggs with this mixture, then garnish with the mock caviare and a band of apple slices.

Turkish Bean Salad

Serves 6

This is called fesulya plaki in Turkey, and is essentially a mix of canned haricot (navy) beans and a helping of Mediterranean vegetables. It's an economical starter and begs for crusty bread on the side.

75 ml/5 tbsp olive oil
2 onions, finely grated
2 garlic cloves, crushed
1 large ripe tomato, blanched, skinned, seeded and chopped
1 green (bell) pepper, seeded and very finely chopped
10 ml/2 tsp caster (superfine) sugar
75 ml/5 tbsp water
2.5–5 ml/½–1 tsp salt
30 ml/2 tbsp chopped dill (dill weed)
400 g/14 oz/1 large can haricot beans, drained

Put the oil, onions and garlic into a 1.75 litre/3 pt/7½ cup dish and cook, uncovered, on Full for 5 minutes, stirring twice. Mix in the tomato, green pepper, sugar, water and salt. Two-thirds cover with a plate and cook on Full for 7 minutes, stirring twice. Allow to cool completely, then cover and chill for several hours. Stir in the dill and beans. Cover again and chill for a further hour.

Bean Salad with Egg

Serves 6

Prepare as for Turkish Bean Salad but garnish each portion with wedges of hard-boiled (hard-cooked) egg.

Potted Kipper

Serves 6

275 g/10 oz kipper fillets
75 g/3 oz/1/3 cup cream cheese
Juice of ½ lemon
2.5 ml/½ tsp English or continental made mustard
1 garlic clove, thinly sliced (optional)
Hot toast or savoury biscuits (crackers), to serve

Microwave the kippers. Remove the skin and bones and flake up the flesh. Transfer to a food processor with the remaining ingredients and process until the mixture forms a paste. Spoon into a small dish and level the top. Cover and chill until firm. Serve spread on to hot toast or savoury biscuits.

Potted Shrimp

Serves 4

Another typically British revivalist recipe. Serve with freshly made thin white toast.

175 g/6 oz/¾ cup unsalted (sweet) butter
225 g/8 oz/2 cups tiny shrimps
A pinch of allspice
White pepper
Toast, to serve

Put the butter into bowl and cover with a plate. Microwave on Full for about 2–3 minutes until melted. Combine two-thirds of the butter with the shrimps, then season with the allspice and pepper to taste. Spoon into four individual pots or ramekin dishes (custard cups). Coat evenly with the rest of the butter. Chill until the butter is set. Turn out on to plates and eat with toast.

Baked Stuffed Egg Avocados

Serves 4

A neglected recipe from the seventies, often chosen then for a light meal or substantial starter.

2 celery stalks, finely chopped
60 ml/4 tbsp fresh white breadcrumbs
2.5 ml/½ tsp finely grated lemon peel
5 ml/1 tsp onion salt
2.5 ml/½ tsp paprika
45 ml/3 tbsp single (light) cream
Freshly ground black pepper
2 medium–large just-ripe avocados
2 large hard-boiled (hard-cooked) eggs, chopped
20 ml/4 tsp toasted breadcrumbs
20 ml/4 tsp melted butter

Combine the celery, white breadcrumbs, lemon peel, onion salt, paprika and cream and add pepper to taste. Halve the avocados and remove the stones (pits). Scoop out some of the flesh to make room for the filling and mash coarsely. Add the flesh to the crumb mixture with the eggs. Mix well and pile into the avocado shells. Arrange on a plate with the pointed ends towards the centre. Sprinkle with the toasted breadcrumbs, then trickle the butter over the top. Cover with kitchen paper and warm on Full for 4–5 minutes. Eat straight away.

Tomato and Cheese-stuffed Avocados

Serves 2 as a main meal, 4 as a starter

A glorious mix, perfect for vegetarians and anyone else thinking along those lines.

2 large ripe avocados
Juice of ½ lime
50 g/2 oz/1 cup soft brown breadcrumbs
1 small onion, finely grated
2 tomatoes, blanched, skinned and chopped
Salt and freshly ground black pepper
50 g/2 oz/½ cup hard cheese, grated
Paprika
8 toasted hazelnuts

Halve the avocados and carefully scoop out the flesh directly into a bowl. Add the lime juice and mash finely with a fork. Stir in the breadcrumbs, onion and tomatoes with salt and pepper to taste. Place in the avocado shells and sprinkle with the cheese and paprika. Top each half with two hazelnuts. Arrange on a large plate with the pointed ends towards the centre. Cover loosely with kitchen paper and cook on Full for 5–5½ minutes. Serve straight away.

Scandinavian Rollmop and Apple Salad

Serves 4

75 g/3 oz dried apple rings
150 ml/¼ pt/2/3 cup water
3 rollmops with onions
150 ml/¼ pt/2/3 cup whipping or double (heavy) cream
Crispbread, to serve

Wash the apple rings, snap into chunks, put into a medium-sized bowl and add the water. Cover with a plate and heat on Full for 5 minutes. Allow to stand for 5 minutes, then drain thoroughly. Undo the rollmops and cut them into diagonal strips. Add to the apple with the onions and mix in the cream. Cover and marinate overnight in the refrigerator. Stir before serving, then arrange on individual plates and serve with crispbread.

Rollmop and Apple Salad with Curry Sauce

Serves 4

Prepare as for Scandinavian Rollmop and Apple Salad, but substitute half mayonnaise and half crème fraîche for the cream. Flavour with curry paste to taste.

Leafy Salad with Goat's Cheese and Warm Dressing

Serves 4

12 small round lettuce leaves
1 box cress
20 rocket leaves
4 individual goat's cheeses
90 ml/6 tbsp grapeseed oil
30 ml/2 tbsp hazelnut oil
10 ml/2 tsp orange flower water
10 ml/2 tsp Dijon mustard
45 ml/3 tbsp rice or cider vinegar
10 ml/2 tsp caster (superfine) sugar
5 ml/1 tsp salt

Wash and dry the lettuce leaves. Trim, wash and dry the cress. Wash and drain the rocket. Arrange these three attractively on four individual plates and place a cheese in the centre of each. Place all the remaining ingredients in a bowl and heat, uncovered, on Defrost for 3 minutes. Stir to mix, then spoon over each salad.

Jellied Tomato Sundaes

Serves 4

4 tomatoes, blanched, skinned and chopped
5 ml/1 tsp finely chopped fresh root ginger
5 ml/1 tsp finely grated lime peel
20 ml/4 tsp powdered gelatine
750 ml/1¼ pt/3 cups chicken stock
30 ml/2 tbsp tomato purée (paste)
5 ml/1 tsp Worcestershire sauce
5 ml/1 tsp caster (superfine) sugar
5 ml/1 tsp celery salt
20 ml/4 tsp crème fraîche
Toasted sesame seeds, for sprinkling
Cheese biscuits (crackers), to serve

Divide the tomatoes equally between four large wine glasses, then sprinkle with the ginger and lime peel. Put the gelatine into a 1.5 litre/ 2½ pt/6 cup bowl with 75 ml/5 tbsp stock and leave to soften for 5 minutes. Melt, uncovered, on Defrost for about 2 minutes. Stir in the remaining stock with the tomato purée, Worcestershire sauce, sugar and celery salt. Whisk gently until evenly combined, then chill only until just beginning to thicken slightly. Spoon over the tomatoes, then chill to set. Top each with 5 ml/1 tsp crème fraîche and a sprinkling of sesame seeds before serving with cheese biscuits.

Stuffed Tomatoes

Serves 4

A sound but uncomplicated starter, delicious served on rounds of buttered toast or rounds of bread fried (sautéed) in garlic butter.

6 tomatoes
1 onion, grated
50 g/2 oz/1 cup fresh white breadcrumbs
5 ml/1 tsp made mustard
5 ml/1 tsp salt
15 ml/1 tbsp chopped chives or parsley
50 g/2 oz/½ cup chopped cold cooked meat or poultry, chopped prawns (shrimp) or grated cheese
1 small egg, beaten

Halve the tomatoes and scoop the centres into a bowl, discarding the hard cores. Stand the shells upside-down on kitchen paper to drain. Put all the remaining ingredients into a bowl and add the tomato pulp. Stir well with a fork to mix, then spoon back into the tomato halves. Arrange in two rings, one inside the other, round the edge of a dinner plate. Cover with kitchen paper and cook on Full for 7 minutes, turning the plate three times. Serve hot, allowing three halves per portion.

Italian Stuffed Tomatoes

Serves 4

6 tomatoes

75 g/3 oz/1½ cups fresh brown breadcrumbs

175 g/6 oz/1½ cups Mozzarella cheese, grated

2.5 ml/½ tsp dried oregano

2.5 ml/½ tsp salt

10 ml/2 tsp chopped basil leaves

1 garlic clove, crushed

1 small egg, beaten

Halve the tomatoes and scoop the centres into a bowl, discarding the hard cores. Stand the shells upside-down on kitchen paper to drain. Put all the remaining ingredients into a bowl and add the tomato pulp. Stir well with a fork to mix, then spoon back into the tomato halves. Arrange in two rings, one inside the other, round the edge of a dinner plate. Cover with kitchen paper and cook on Full for 7–8 minutes, turning the plate three times. Serve hot or cold, allowing three halves per portion.

Tomato and Chicken Salad Cups

Serves 4

450 ml/¾ pt/2 cups chicken stock
15 ml/1 tbsp powdered gelatine
30 ml/2 tbsp tomato purée (paste)
1 small onion, finely grated
5 ml/1 tsp caster (superfine) sugar
1 small green (bell) pepper, cut into tiny cubes
175 g/6 oz/1½ cups cold cooked meat, finely chopped
1 carrot, grated
2 canned pineapple rings (not fresh or the jelly won't set)
2 hard-boiled (hard-cooked) eggs, grated

Pour half the stock into a 1.5 litre/ 2½ pt/6 cup bowl. Stir in the gelatine and leave to soften for 5 minutes. Melt, uncovered, on Defrost for 2–2½ minutes. Add the remaining stock, stirring well to mix. Cover and chill until cold and just beginning to thicken, then fold in all the remaining ingredients except the eggs. Divide between four glass bowls and chill until set. Before serving, sprinkle with the egg.

Chopped Egg and Onion

Serves 4 as a starter, 6 as an appetiser

A spectacular all-year-round Jewish classic, best eaten with crisp biscuits such as traditional matzos. The big advantage is microwaving the eggs – no steamed-up kitchen and no saucepan to wash up. Butter or any margarine is suggested here, but the orthodox community would use only vegetable margarine.

5 hard-boiled (hard-cooked) eggs, shelled and finely chopped
40 g/1½ oz/3 tbsp butter or margarine, softened
1 onion, finely grated
Salt and freshly ground black pepper
Salad leaves or parsley, to garnish

Combine the chopped eggs with the butter or margarine. Stir in the onion and season to taste. Pile on to four plates and garnish each with salad leaves or parsley.

Quiche Lorraine

Serves 4–6

The original French quiche or savoury flan, with a 'family' of variations.

For the pastry (paste):
175 g/6 oz/1½ cups plain (all-purpose) flour
1.5 ml/¼ tsp salt
100 g/3½ oz/scant ½ cup butter mixed with margarine, white cooking fat or lard, or use all margarine
1 small egg yolk
For the filling:
6 rashers (slices) streaky bacon
3 eggs
300 ml/½ pt/1¼ cups full-cream milk or single (light) cream
2.5 ml/½ level tsp salt
Freshly ground black pepper
Grated nutmeg

To make the pastry, sift the flour and salt into a bowl. Rub in the fat until the mixture resembles fine breadcrumbs, then mix to a firm dough with cold water. Wrap in foil and chill for ½–¾ hour. Turn out on to a floured surface and knead quickly and lightly until smooth. Roll out into a thin circle and use to line a 20 cm/8 in diameter glass, china or pottery flan dish. Pinch the top edge into tiny flutes, then prick all over with fork. Cook uncovered on Full for 6 minutes, turning the dish twice. If the pastry has bulged in places, press down gently with a hand protected by an oven glove. Brush all over with the egg yolk and cook on Full for 1 minute to seal any holes. Leave to stand while preparing the filling.

Arrange the bacon rashers on a plate lined with kitchen paper, cover with another sheet of kitchen paper and cook on Full for 5 minutes, turning once. Drain and allow to cool slightly. Cut each rasher into three pieces and place over the base of the pastry case. Beat the eggs with the milk or cream and season with the salt and pepper to taste. Strain carefully into the flan over the bacon and sprinkle with nutmeg. Cook uncovered on Full, turning the dish four times, for 10–12 minutes or until bubbles just begin to break across the centre. Allow to stand for 10 minutes before cutting. Eat warm or cold.

Cheese and Tomato Quiche

Serves 4–6

Prepare as for Quiche Lorraine, but substitute three skinned and sliced tomatoes for the bacon.

Smoked Salmon Quiche

Serves 4–6

Prepare as for Quiche Lorraine, but substitute 175 g/6 oz smoked salmon, cut into strips, for the bacon.

Prawn Quiche

Serves 4–6

Prepare as for Quiche Lorraine, but substitute 175 g/6 oz/1½ cups chopped prawns (shrimp) for the bacon.

Spinach Quiche

Serves 4–6

Prepare as for Quiche Lorraine, but cover the base of the flan with 175 g/6 oz cooked spinach, from which all the water has been wrung out, instead of the bacon. (The spinach must be as dry as possible or the pastry (paste) will become soggy.)

Mediterranean Quiche

Serves 4–6

Prepare as for Quiche Lorraine, but cover the base of the flan with 185 g/6½ oz/1 small can flaked tuna and its oil, 12 stoned (pitted) black olives and 20 ml/4 tsp tomato purée (paste) instead of the bacon.

Asparagus Quiche

Serves 4–6

Prepare as for Quiche Lorraine, but substitute 350 g/12 oz/1 large can asparagus spears for the bacon. Drain thoroughly, reserve six spears and chop the remainder. Use to cover the base of the flan. Garnish with the reserved spears.

Devilled Walnuts

Serves 4–6

225 g/8 oz/2 cups walnut halves
50 g/2 oz/¼ cup butter
10 ml/2 tsp corn oil
5 ml/1 tsp mustard powder
5 ml/1 tsp paprika
5 ml/1 tsp celery salt
5 ml/1 tsp onion salt
2.5 ml/½ tsp chilli powder
Salt

Toast the walnut halves. Heat the butter and oil in a shallow dish, uncovered, on Full for 1½ minutes. Add the nuts and toss gently with the butter and oil until well mixed. Leave uncovered and cook on Full for 3–4 minutes, turning often and watching carefully in case they start to over-brown. Drain on kitchen paper. Toss in a plastic bag with the mustard powder, paprika, celery salt, onion salt, chilli powder and salt to taste. Store in an airtight container.

Curried Brazil Nuts

Serves 4–6

225 g/8 oz/2 cups brazil nuts, thickly sliced
50 g/2 oz/¼ cup butter
10 ml/2 tsp corn oil
20 ml/4 tsp mild, medium or hot curry powder
Salt

Toast the brazil nuts. Heat the butter and oil in a shallow dish, uncovered, on Full for 1½ minutes. Add the nuts and toss gently with the butter and oil until well mixed. Leave uncovered and cook on Full for 3–4 minutes, turning often and watching carefully in case they start to over-brown. Drain on kitchen paper. Toss in a plastic bag with the curry powder and salt to taste. Store in an airtight container.

Blue Cheese and Pecan Flan

Serves 4–6

A sophisticated addition to the quiche family.

For the pastry (paste):
175 g/6 oz/1½ cups plain (all-purpose) flour
1.5 ml/¼ tsp salt
100 g/3½ oz/scant ½ cup butter mixed with margarine, white cooking fat or lard, or use all margarine
45 ml/3 tbsp finely chopped pecan nuts
1 small egg yolk

For the filling:
200 g/7 oz/scant 1 cup full-fat cream cheese
30–45 ml/2–3 tbsp snipped chives or spring onions (scallions)
125 g/4 oz/generous 1 cup blue cheese, crumbled
5 ml/1 tsp paprika
3 eggs
60 ml/4 tbsp full-cream milk or single (light) cream
Salt and freshly ground black pepper

To make the pastry, sift the flour and salt into a bowl. Rub in the fat until the mixture resembles fine breadcrumbs, then add the chopped nuts. Mix to a firm dough with cold water. Wrap in foil and chill for ½–¾ hour. Turn out on to a floured surface and knead quickly and lightly until smooth. Roll out into a thin circle and use to line a 20 cm/8 in diameter glass, china or pottery flan dish. Pinch the top edge into tiny flutes, then prick all over with a fork. Cook uncovered on Full for 6 minutes, turning the dish twice. If the pastry has bulged in places, press down gently with a hand protected by an oven glove. Brush all over with the egg yolk and cook on Full for 1 minute to seal any holes. Leave to stand while preparing the filling.

Put the filling ingredients into a food processor, seasoning to taste with salt and pepper, and process until the mixture is smooth. Spread smoothly into the flan case (pie shell). Cook on Defrost for 14 minutes, turning the dish three times. Allow to stand for 5 minutes. Eat warm or cold.

Rich Liver Pâté

Serves 8–10

Excellent served with hot toast at parties or special dinners.

250 g/9 oz/generous 1 cup butter
1 garlic clove, crushed
450 g/1 lb chicken livers
1.5 ml/¼ tsp grated nutmeg
Salt and freshly ground black pepper

Put 175 g/6 oz/¾ cup of the butter into a 1.75 litre/3 pt/7½ cup dish and melt, uncovered, on Full for 2 minutes. Stir in the garlic. Pierce each piece of chicken liver with the tip of a knife and add to the dish. Mix well with the butter. Cover with a plate and cook on Full for 8 minutes, stirring twice. Mix in the nutmeg, then season well to taste. In two batc

Hot and Sour Crab Soup

Serves 6

An opulent contribution from China, an easily made pleasure.

1 litre/1¾ pts/4¼ cups poultry stock
225 g/7 oz/1 small can water chestnuts, coarsely chopped
225 g/7 oz/1 small can sliced bamboo shoots in water
75 g/3 oz mushrooms, thinly sliced
150 g/5 oz tofu, cut into small cubes
175 g/6 oz/1 small can crabmeat in brine, undrained and meat flaked
15 ml/1 tbsp cornflour
15 ml/1 tbsp water
30 ml/2 tbsp malt vinegar
15 ml/1 tbsp soy sauce
5 ml/1 tsp sesame oil
2.5 ml/½ tsp salt
1 large egg, beaten

Pour the stock into a 2 litre/3½ pt/ 8½ cup bowl. Add the contents of the cans of water chestnuts and bamboo shoots. Add the mushrooms and tofu and the contents of the can of crabmeat. Stir. Cover the bowl with clingfilm (plastic wrap) and slit it twice to allow steam to escape. Cook on Full for 15 minutes. Uncover carefully to prevent steam burns and stir well to mix. Blend the cornflour smoothly with the water and vinegar, then stir in the remaining ingredients. Gently whisk into the soup. Cover as before and cook on Full for 4 minutes. Stir round and cover with large plate or saucepan lid. Allow to stand for 2 minutes. Serve hot in china bowls.

Easy Oriental Soup

Serves 3–4

400 ml/16 fl oz/1 large can mulligatawny soup
400 ml/16 fl oz/1 large can coconut milk
Salt
Chilli powder
Chopped coriander (cilantro)
Popadoms, to serve

Pour the soup and coconut milk into a 1.75 litre/3 pt/7½ cup bowl. Add salt to taste. Heat, uncovered, on Full for 7–8 minutes, stirring twice. Pour into warm bowls, sprinkle with chilli powder and coriander and serve with popadoms.

Liver Dumpling Soup

Serves 4

50 g/2 oz/1 cup fresh white breadcrumbs
50 g/2 oz/½ cup chicken livers, minced (ground)
15 ml/1 tbsp very finely chopped parsley, plus extra to garnish
5 ml/1 tsp grated onion
1.5 ml/¼ tsp marjoram
1.5 ml/¼ tsp salt
Freshly ground black pepper
½ egg, beaten
750 ml/1¼ pts/3 cups clear beef or chicken stock or diluted canned concentrated consommé

Place all the ingredients, except the stock or consommé, into a mixing bowl. Mix thoroughly and shape into 12 small dumplings. Pour the stock or consommé into a deep 1.5 litre/2½ pt/ 6 cup bowl and cover with a plate. Heat on Full to boiling, allowing about 8–10 minutes. Add the dumplings. Cook, uncovered, for 3–4 minutes until the dumplings have risen and float to the top of the soup. Ladle into warm bowls, sprinkle with the extra parsley and serve straight away.

Cream of Carrot Soup

Serves 6

30 ml/2 tbsp cornflour (cornstarch)
550 g/1¼ lb/1 large can carrots
450 ml/¾ pt/2 cups cold milk
7.5–10 ml/1½–2 tsp salt
300 ml/½ pt/1¼ cups hot water
60 ml/4 tbsp single (light) cream

Place the cornflour in a 3 litre/5¼ pt/ 12 cup bowl. Mix smoothly with the liquid from the can of carrots. Blend the carrots to a purée in a blender or food processor. Add to the bowl with the milk and salt. Cook, uncovered, on Full for 12 minutes until thickened, whisking gently four or five times to ensure smoothness. Thin down with the hot water. Spoon into warmed bowls and swirl 10 ml/2 tsp cream into each portion.

Chilled Carrot and Leek Soup

Serves 6

1 large leek, slit and thoroughly washed
4 large carrots, thinly sliced
3 small–medium potatoes, cut into small cubes
150 ml/¼ pt/⅔ cup hot water
600 ml/1 pt/2½ cups vegetable stock
300 ml/½ pt/1¼ cups single (light) cream
Salt and freshly ground black pepper
Chopped watercress

Coarsely chop the leek. Put all the vegetables in a 2 litre/3½ pt/8½ cup dish with the hot water. Cover with clingfilm (plastic wrap) and slit it twice to allow steam to escape. Cook on Full for 15 minutes until the vegetables are tender. Transfer to a blender or food processor with the liquid from the dish and work to a smooth purée, adding a little of the stock if necessary. Scrape into a large bowl and stir in the remaining stock. Cover and chill. Before serving, gently whisk in the cream and season to taste. Ladle into soup cups and sprinkle each with cress.

Carrot and Coriander Soup

Serves 6

Prepare as for Cream of Carrot Soup, but add a handful of fresh coriander (cilantro) leaves to the blender or food processor with the carrots. The cream can be added as an optional extra.

Carrot with Orange Soup

Serves 6

Prepare as for Cream of Carrot Soup, but add 10 ml/2 tsp grated orange peel to the soup half-way through cooking. Top each portion with whipped cream to which a little Grand Marnier has been added.

Lettuce Cream Soup

Serves 6

75 g/3 oz/1/3 cup butter or margarine
2 onions, grated
225 g/8 oz round soft lettuce, cut into strips
600 ml/1 pt/2½ cups full-cream milk
30 ml/2 tbsp cornflour (cornstarch)
300 ml/½ pt/1¼ cups hot water or vegetable stock
2.5 ml/½ tsp salt

Melt 50 g/2 oz/¼ cup of the butter or margarine in a 1.75 litre/ 3 pt/7½ cup bowl on Defrost for 2 minutes. Mix in the onions and lettuce. Cover with a plate and cook on Full for 3½ minutes. Transfer to a blender with one-third of the milk. Work to a smooth purée. Return to the bowl. Mix the cornflour smoothly with 60 ml/ 4 tbsp of the remaining milk. Add to the soup with all the remaining milk, the hot water or stock and the salt. Cook, uncovered, on Full for 15 minutes, whisking frequently to ensure smoothness. Serve in warmed bowls with 5 ml/1 tsp butter added to each.

Green Purée Soup

Serves 4–6

1 large round lettuce
125 g/4 oz watercress or young spinach
1 leek, white part only, sliced
300 ml/½ pt/1¼ cups hot water
60 ml/4 tbsp cornflour (cornstarch)
300 ml/½ pt/1¼ cups cold milk
25 g/1 oz/2 tbsp butter or margarine
Salt
Croûtons, to serve

Thoroughly wash the lettuce and watercress or spinach and shred. Place in a 1.5 litre/2½ pt/6 cup bowl with the leek and water. Cover with clingfilm (plastic wrap) and slit it twice to allow steam to escape. Cook on Full for 10 minutes, turning the bowl twice. Allow to cool for 10 minutes. Transfer to a blender and work to a smooth purée. Return to the bowl. Blend the cornflour smoothly with the milk. Add to the bowl with the butter or margarine and salt to taste. Cook, uncovered, on Full, stirring three times for 8–10 minutes or until piping hot and slightly thickened. Ladle into warmed soup bowls and add croûtons to each.

Parsnip and Parsley Soup with Wasabi

Serves 6

With a subtle kick of horseradish from the wasabi, this is an intriguingly flavoured, highly original soup with just a hint of sweetness from the parsnips.

30 ml/2 tbsp corn or sunflower oil
450 g/1 lb parsnips, peeled and sliced
900 ml/1½ pts/3¾ cups well-flavoured hot vegetable or chicken stock
10 ml/2 tsp Japanese wasabi powder
30 ml/2 tbsp chopped parsley
150 ml/¼ pt/2/3 cup single (light) cream

Pour the oil into a 2 litre/3½ pt/ 8½ cup dish. Add the parsnips. Cover with clingfilm (plastic wrap) and slit it twice to allow steam to escape. Cook on Full for 7 minutes, turning the dish twice. Add the stock and wasabi powder. Cover with a plate and cook on Full for 6 minutes. Allow to cool slightly, then purée until smooth in a blender. Return to the bowl. Stir in the parsley. Cover as before and cook on Full for 5 minutes. Stir in the cream and serve.

Sweet Potato Soup

Serves 6

Prepare as for Parsnip and Parsley Soup with Wasabi, but substitute chopped, orange-fleshed sweet potatoes for the parsnips.

Cream of Vegetable Soup

Serves 4–6

A very useful soup – use any combination of vegetables you fancy or have available.

450 g/1 lb mixed fresh vegetables
1 onion, chopped
25 g/1 oz/2 tbsp butter or margarine or 30 ml/2 tbsp sunflower oil
175 ml/6 fl oz/¾ cup water
450 ml/¾ pt/2 cups milk or milk and water mixed
15 ml/1 tbsp cornflour (cornstarch)
2.5 ml/½ tsp salt
Chopped parsley

Prepare the vegetables according to type and cut into small pieces. Put into 2 litre/3½ pt/8½ cup bowl with the onion, butter, margarine or oil and 30 ml/2 tbsp of the water. Cover with a plate and cook on Full for 12–14 minutes until tender, stirring four times. Purée until smooth in a blender. Return to the bowl with three-quarters of the milk or milk and water. Mix the cornflour smoothly with the remaining liquid and add to the bowl with the salt. Cook, uncovered, on Full for 6 minutes, stirring four times. Ladle into soup bowls and sprinkle each with parsley.

Green Pea Soup

Serves 4–6

Prepare as for Cream of Vegetable Soup, but substitute 450 g/1 lb frozen garden peas for the mixed vegetables and onion. Garnish lightly with chopped mint instead of parsley.

Squash Soup

Serves 4–6

Prepare as for Cream of Vegetable Soup, but substitute 450 g/1 lb peeled and diced courgettes (zucchini), marrow, pumpkin, butternut or turban squash for the mixed vegetables and onion. Sprinkle each serving with grated nutmeg instead of parsley.

Cream of Mushroom Soup

Serves 4–6

Prepare as for Cream of Vegetable Soup, but substitute mushrooms for the mixed vegetables and onion.

Cream of Pumpkin Soup

Serves 6–8

For Hallowe'en mostly, but the soup is glorious chilled so freeze any leftovers, or make an extra batch while pumpkins are in season, and keep for the beginning of summer.

1.75 kg/4 lb fresh pumpkin, either in the piece or a whole one
2 onions, coarsely chopped
15–20 ml/3–4 tsp salt
600 ml/1 pt/2½ cups full-cream milk
15 ml/1 tbsp cornflour (cornstarch)
30 ml/2 tbsp cold water
2.5 ml/½ tsp grated nutmeg
Croûtons, to serve (optional)

Cut the pumpkin into wedges like melon. Remove the seeds and wash and dry them. Arrange on a plate in a single layer. Toast lightly, uncovered, on Full for 4 minutes. Allow to cool, then crack open the husks and remove the inside seeds. Reserve. Peel the pumpkin and cut the flesh into fairly large cubes. Put into a large bowl with the onions and toss well to mix. Cover closely with clingfilm (plastic wrap) but do not slit. Cook on Full for 30 minutes, turning the bowl four times. Remove from the oven and allow to stand for 10 minutes. Work the pumpkin, onions and cooking liquid to a purée, in several batches, in a blender or food processor. Return to the bowl. Stir in the salt and milk.

Mix the cornflour smoothly with the water and add to the purée with the nutmeg. Reheat, uncovered, on Full for 7 minutes, whisking every minute. Ladle the soup into bowls or cups and sprinkle with the toasted pumpkin seeds and/or croûtons.

Cock-a-leekie Soup

Serves 6–8

4 chicken portions
4 leeks, coarsely shredded
1.25 litre/2¼ pts/5½ cups hot water
10 ml/2 tsp salt
1 bouquet garni sachet
50 g/2 oz/¼ cup easy-cook long-grain rice
12 stoned (pitted) prunes

Wash the chicken and place in a 20 cm/8 in diameter deep casserole dish (Dutch oven). Add the leeks. Cover with clingfilm (plastic wrap) and slit it twice to allow steam to escape. Cook on Full for 12 minutes. Lift the chicken out of the dish, remove the meat from the bones and cut into bite-sized pieces. Reserve. Pour the water into a second, large dish. Add the salt and bouquet garni with the rice, leeks and the liquid from the casserole dish. Cover with a plate and cook on Full for 18 minutes. Stir in the chicken and prunes. Cover as before and cook for a further 3 minutes. Eat while very hot.

Scotch Broth

Serves 6

30 ml/2 tbsp pearl barley
225 g/8 oz neck of lamb fillet, cut into bite-sized cubes
1.2 litres/2 pts/5 cups hot water
1 large onion, chopped
1 carrot, cut into small cubes
1 small turnip, cut into small cubes
1 small leek, shredded
Salt and freshly ground black pepper
Chopped parsley

Soak the barley for 4 hours in 75 ml/ 5 tbsp cold water. Drain. Place the lamb in a 2.25 litre/4 pt/10 cup bowl. Add the hot water and barley. Cover with a plate and cook on Full for 4 minutes. Skim. Add the prepared vegetables and salt and pepper to taste. Cover as before and cook on Full for 25–30 minutes until the barley is soft. Allow to stand for 5 minutes. Ladle into warmed soup bowls and sprinkle each thickly with parsley.

Israeli Chicken and Avocado Soup

Serves 4–5

900 ml/1½ pts/3¾ cups well-flavoured chicken stock
1 large ripe avocado, peeled and stoned
30 ml/2 tbsp fresh lemon juice

Pour the chicken stock into a 1.5 litre/2½ pt/6 cup bowl. Cover with a plate and heat on Full for 9 minutes. Mash the avocado flesh with the lemon juice to a coarse purée. Stir into the hot stock. Cover as before and reheat on Full for 1 minute. Serve hot.

Avocado Soup with Beetroot

Serves 4–5

Prepare as for Israeli Chicken and Avocado Soup and garnish each portion with 7.5 ml/1½ tsp grated cooked beetroot (red beets).

Bortsch

Serves 6

450 g/1 lb raw beetroot (red beets)
75 ml/5 tbsp water
1 large carrot, peeled and grated
1 small turnip, peeled and grated
1 onion, peeled and grated
750 ml/1¼ pts/3 cups hot beef or vegetable stock
125 g/4 oz white cabbage, shredded
15 ml/1 tbsp lemon juice
5 ml/1 tsp salt
Freshly ground black pepper
90 ml/6 tbsp soured (dairy sour) cream

Wash the beetroot thoroughly but leave unpeeled. Place in a shallow 20 cm/ 8 in diameter dish, in a single layer, with the water. Cover with clingfilm (plastic wrap) and slit it twice to allow steam to escape. Cook on Full for 15 minutes. Place the carrot, tur-nip and onion in a 2 litre/3½ pt/ 8½ cup bowl. Drain and peel the beetroot and slice. Add to the bowl of vegetables with 150 ml/¼ pt/2/3 cup stock. Cover as before and cook on Full for 10 minutes. Mix in the remaining stock and all the remaining ingredients except the soured cream, seasoning to taste. Cover with a plate and cook on Full for 10 minutes, stirring four times. Ladle into warmed soup bowls and top each with 15 ml/1 tbsp soured cream.

Cold Bortsch

Serves 6

Prepare as for Bortsch and allow to cool. Strain when cold. Add 150 ml/ ¼ pt/2/3 cup cold water and 1 large cooked beetroot, coarsely shredded. Allow to stand for 15 minutes. Strain again. Sharpen with extra lemon juice to taste. Chill for several hours before serving.

Creamy Cold Bortsch

Serves 6

Prepare as for Cold Bortsch. After the second straining, blend in a blender or food processor with 250 ml/ 8 fl oz/1 cup half-fat crème fraîche. Chill.

Orange Lentil Soup

Serves 4–5

125 g/4 oz/½ cup orange lentils
1 large onion, grated
1 large carrot, grated
½ small turnip, grated
1 potato, grated
20 ml/4 tsp butter or margarine
5 ml/1 tsp corn or sunflower oil
30 ml/2 tbsp chopped parsley, plus extra for garnishing
900 ml/1½ pts/3¾ cups hot chicken or vegetable stock
Salt and freshly ground black pepper

Wash and drain the lentils. Place the vegetables, butter or margarine and oil in a 2 litre/3½ pt/8½ cup bowl. Add the parsley. Cook, uncovered, on Full for 5 minutes, stirring three times. Stir in the lentils and one-third of the hot stock. Season to taste. Cover with clingfilm (plastic wrap) and slit it twice to allow steam to escape. Cook on Full for 10 minutes until the lentils are tender. (If not, cook for a further 5–6 minutes.) Transfer to a blender or food processor and work to a coarse purée. Return to the bowl with the remaining stock. Cover with a plate and reheat on Full for 6 minutes, stirring three times. Serve straight away, sprinkling each portion with extra parsley.

Orange Lentil Soup with Cheese and Toasted Cashews

Serves 4–5

Prepare as for Orange Lentil Soup, but stir in 60 ml/4 tbsp grated Edam cheese and 60 ml/4 tbsp coarsely chopped toasted cashew nuts after the final reheating.

Lentil Soup with Tomato Garnish

Serves 4–5

Prepare as for Orange Lentil Soup, but instead of sprinkling with parsley, top each portion with 5 ml/1 tsp sun-dried tomato paste, then float in a slice of fresh tomato.

Yellow Pea Soup

Serves 6–8

A Swedish version of pea soup, eaten every Thursday in Sweden. It is customarily followed by pancakes and jam.

350 g/12 oz/1½ cups yellow split peas, washed

900 ml/1½ pts/3¾ cups cold water

5 ml/1 tsp marjoram

1 ham bone, about 450–500 g/1 lb

750 ml/1¼ pts/3 cups hot water

5–10 ml/1–2 tsp salt

Place the split peas in a mixing bowl. Add the cold water. Cover with a plate and cook on Full for 6 minutes. Allow to stand for 3 hours. Transfer the peas and soaking water to a 2.5 litre/ 4½ pt/11 cup bowl. Stir in the marjoram and add the ham bone. Cover with clingfilm (plastic wrap) and slit it twice to allow steam to escape. Cook on Full for 30 minutes. Mix in half the hot water. Cover as before and cook on Full for a further 15 minutes. Remove the bone. Take the meat off the bone and cut it into small pieces. Return to the soup with the remaining hot water. Season to taste with the salt. Stir well. Cover with a plate and reheat on Full for 3 minutes. The soup can be thinned, if preferred, with extra boiling water.

French Onion Soup

Serves 6

30 ml/2 tbsp butter, margarine or sunflower oil
4 onions, thinly sliced and separated into rings
20 ml/4 tsp cornflour (cornstarch)
900 ml/1½ pts/3¾ cups hot beef stock or consommé
Salt and freshly ground black pepper
6 slices French bread, diagonally sliced
90 ml/6 tbsp grated Gruyère (Swiss) or Jarlsberg cheese
Paprika

Place the butter, margarine or oil in a 2 litre/3½ pt/8½ cup dish. Heat, uncovered, on Full for 2 minutes. Stir the onion rings into the dish. Cook, uncovered, on Full for 5 minutes. Stir in the cornflour. Gradually blend in half the hot stock. Cover the dish with clingfilm (plastic wrap) and slit it twice to allow steam to escape. Cook on Full for 30 minutes, turning the dish four times. Mix in the remaining stock and season to taste. Stir well. Ladle the soup into six bowls and add a slice of bread to each. Sprinkle with the cheese and paprika. Return each bowl individually to the microwave and heat on Full for 1½ minutes until the cheese is melted and bubbling. Eat straight away.

Minestrone

Serves 8–10

350 g/12 oz courgettes (zucchini), thinly sliced
225 g/8 oz carrots, thinly sliced
225 g/8 oz onions, coarsely chopped
125 g/4 oz white cabbage, shredded
125 g/4 oz green cabbage, shredded
3 celery stalks, thinly sliced
3 potatoes, cubed
125 g/4 oz/1 cup fresh or frozen peas
125 g/4 oz fresh or frozen sliced green beans
400 g/14 oz/1 large can tomatoes
30 ml/2 tbsp tomato purée (paste)
50 g/2 oz macaroni, broken into short lengths
1 litre/1¾ pts/4¼ cup hot water
15–20 ml/3–4 tsp salt
100 g/3½ oz/1 cup grated Parmesan cheese

Place all the prepared vegetables in a 3.5 litre/6 pt/15 cup bowl. Stir in the remaining ingredients except the water and salt, breaking up the tomatoes against the side of the bowl with the back of a wooden spoon. Cover with a large plate and cook on Full for 15 minutes, stirring three times. Mix in about three-quarters of the hot water. Cover as before and cook on Full for 25 minutes, stirring four or five times. Remove from the microwave. Stir in the remaining water and the salt to taste. If the soup seems too thick, dilute with extra boiling water. Ladle into deep bowls and serve with the Parmesan cheese handed separately.

Minestrone Genovese

Serves 8–10

Prepare as for Minestrone, but stir in 30 ml/2 tbsp ready-prepared green pesto before serving.

Italian Potato Soup

Serves 4–5

1 large onion, chopped
30 ml/2 tbsp olive or sunflower oil
4 large potatoes
1 small cooked ham bone
1.25 litres/2¼ pts/5½ cups hot chicken stock
Salt and freshly ground black pepper
60 ml/4 tbsp single (light) cream
Grated nutmeg
30 ml/2 tbsp chopped parsley

Place the onion and oil in a 2.25 litre/4 pt/10 cup bowl. Cook, uncovered, on Defrost for 5 minutes, stirring twice. Meanwhile, peel and grate the potatoes. Stir into the onions and add the ham bone, hot stock and salt and pepper to taste. Cover with a plate and cook on Full for 15–20 minutes, stirring twice, until the potatoes are soft. Mix in the cream, ladle into soup bowls and sprinkle with nutmeg and the parsley.

Fresh Tomato and Celery Soup

Serves 6–8

900 g/2 lb ripe tomatoes, blanched, skinned and quartered
50 g/2 oz/¼ cup butter or margarine or 30 ml/2 tbsp olive oil
2 celery stalks, finely chopped
1 large onion, finely chopped
30 ml/2 tbsp dark soft brown sugar
5 ml/1 tsp soy sauce
2.5 ml/½ tsp salt
300 ml/½ pt/1¼ cups hot water
30 ml/2 tbsp cornflour (cornstarch)
150 ml/¼ pt/2/3 cup cold water
Medium sherry

Purée the tomatoes in a blender or food processor. Place the butter, margarine or oil in a 1.75 litre/3 pt/ 7½ cup dish. Heat on Full for 1 minute. Mix in the celery and onion. Cover with a plate and cook on Full for 3 minutes. Add the puréed tomatoes, sugar, soy sauce, salt and hot water. Cover as before and cook on Full for 8 minutes, stirring four times. Meanwhile, mix the cornflour smoothly with the cold water. Stir into the soup. Cook, uncovered, on Full for 8 minutes, stirring four times. Ladle into soup bowls and add a dash of sherry to each.

Tomato Soup with Avocado Dressing

Serves 8

2 ripe avocados
Juice of 1 small lime
1 garlic clove, crushed
30 ml/2 tbsp mustard mayonnaise
45 ml/3 tbsp crème fraîche
5 ml/1 tsp salt
A pinch of turmeric
600 ml/20 fl oz/2 cans condensed tomato soup
600 ml/1 pt/2½ cups warm water
2 tomatoes, blanched, skinned, seeded and quartered

Peel and halve the avocados, removing the stones (pits). Finely mash the flesh, then combine with the lime juice, garlic, mayonnaise, crème fraîche, salt and turmeric. Cover and chill until needed. Pour both cans of soup into a 1.75 litre/3 pt/7½ cup dish. Gently whisk in the water. Cut the tomato flesh into strips and add two-thirds to the soup. Cover the dish with a plate and cook on Full for 9 minutes until very hot, stirring four or five times. Ladle into soup bowls and add a scoop of avocado dressing to each. Garnish with the remaining tomato strips.

Chilled Cheese and Onion Soup

Serves 6–8

25 g/1 oz/2 tbsp butter or margarine
2 onions, chopped
2 celery stalks, finely chopped
30 ml/2 tbsp plain (all-purpose) flour
900 ml/1½ pts/3¾ cups warm chicken or vegetable stock
45 ml/3 tbsp dry white wine or white port
Salt and freshly ground black pepper
125 g/4 oz/1 cup blue cheese, crumbled
125 g/4 oz/1 cup Cheddar cheese, grated
150 ml/¼ pt/2/3 cup whipping cream
Finely chopped sage, to garnish

Place the butter or margarine in a 2.25 litre/4 pt/10 cup dish. Melt, uncovered, on Defrost for 1½ minutes. Mix in the onions and celery. Cover with a plate and cook on Full for 8 minutes. Remove from the microwave. Stir in the flour, then gradually blend in the stock and wine or port. Cover as before and cook on Full for 10–12 minutes, whisking every 2–3 minutes, until the soup is smooth, thickened and hot. Season to taste. Add the cheeses and stir until melted. Cover and allow to cool, then chill for several hours or overnight. Before serving, stir round and gently whisk in the cream. Ladle into cups or bowls and sprinkle each lightly with sage.

Swiss-style Cheese Soup

Serves 6–8

25 g/1 oz/2 tbsp butter or margarine
2 onions, chopped
2 celery stalks, finely chopped
30 ml/2 tbsp plain (all-purpose) flour
900 ml/1½ pts/3¾ cups warm chicken or vegetable stock
45 ml/3 tbsp dry white wine or white port
5 ml/1 tsp caraway seeds
1 garlic clove, crushed
Salt and freshly ground black pepper
225 g/8 oz/2 cups Emmental or Gruyère (Swiss) cheese, grated
150 ml/¼ pt/2/3 cup whipping cream
Croûtons

Place the butter or margarine in a 2.25 litre/4 pt/10 cup dish. Melt, uncovered, on Defrost for 1½ minutes. Mix in the onions and celery. Cover with a plate and cook on Full for 8 minutes. Remove from the microwave. Stir in the flour, then gradually blend in the stock and wine or port. Stir in the caraway seeds and garlic. Cover as before and cook on Full for 10–12 minutes, whisking every 2–3 minutes, until the soup is hot, smooth and thickened. Season to taste. Add the cheese and stir until melted. Mix in the cream. Ladle into cups or bowls and serve hot, garnished with croûtons.

Avgolemono Soup

Serves 6

1.25 litres/2¼ pts/5½ cups hot chicken stock
60 ml/4 tbsp risotto rice
Juice of 2 lemons
2 large eggs
Salt and freshly ground black pepper

Pour the stock into a deep 1.75 litre/ 3 pt/7½ cup dish. Stir in the rice. Cover with a plate and cook on Full for 20–25 minutes until the rice is tender. Thoroughly beat together the lemon juice and eggs in a soup tureen or other large serving dish. Gently whisk in the stock and rice. Season to taste before serving.

Cream of Cucumber Soup with Pastis

Serves 6–8

900 g/2 lb cucumber, peeled
45 ml/3 tbsp butter or margarine
30 ml/2 tbsp cornflour (cornstarch)
600 ml/1 pt/2½ cups chicken or vegetable stock
300 ml/½ pt/1¼ cups whipping cream
7.5–10 ml/1½–2 tsp salt
10 ml/2 tsp Pernod or Ricard (pastis)
Freshly ground black pepper
Chopped dill (dill weed)

Slice the cucumber very thinly using a grater or the slicing disc of a food processor. Place in a bowl, cover and leave to stand for 30 minutes to allow some of the moisture to seep out. Wring as dry as possible in a clean tea towel (dish cloth). Place the butter or margarine in a 2.25 litre/4 pt/10 cup dish. Melt, uncovered, on Defrost for 1½ minutes. Mix in the cucumber. Cover with a plate and cook on Full for 5 minutes, stirring three times. Mix the cornflour smoothly with some of the stock, then add the remaining stock. Gradually stir into the cucumber. Cook, uncovered, on Full for about 8 minutes, stirring three or four times, until the soup is hot, smooth and thickened. Add the cream, salt and pastis and mix thoroughly. Reheat, uncovered, on Full for 1–1½ minutes. Season to taste with pepper. Ladle into soup bowls and sprinkle each portion with dill.

Curry Soup with Rice

Serves 6

A pleasantly mild Anglo-Indian chicken soup.

30 ml/2 tbsp groundnut or sunflower oil
1 large onion, chopped
3 celery stalks, finely chopped
15 ml/1 tbsp mild curry powder
30 ml/2 tbsp medium-dry sherry
1 litre/1¾ pts/4¼ cups chicken or vegetable stock
125 g/4 oz/½ cup long-grain rice
5 ml/1 tsp salt
15 ml/1 tbsp soy sauce
175 g/6 oz/1½ cups cooked chicken, cut into strips
Thick plain yoghurt or crème fraîche, to serve

Pour the oil into a 2.25 litre/4 pt/ 10 cup dish. Heat, uncovered, on Full for 1 minute. Add the onions and celery. Cook, uncovered, on Full for 5 minutes, stirring once. Mix in the curry powder, sherry, stock, rice, salt and soy sauce. Cover with a plate and cook on Full for 10 minutes, stirring twice. Add the chicken. Cover as before and cook on Full for 6 minutes. Ladle into bowls and top each with a swirl of yoghurt or crème fraîche.

Vichyssoise

Serves 6

An up-market and chilled version of leek and potato soup, invented by the American chef Louis Diat early in the twentieth century.

2 leeks
350 g/12 oz potatoes, peeled and sliced
25 g/1 oz/2 tbsp butter or margarine
30 ml/2 tbsp water
450 ml/¾ pt/2 cups milk
15 ml/1 tbsp cornflour (cornstarch)
150 ml/¼ pt/2/3 cup cold water
2.5 ml/½ tsp salt
150 ml/¼ pt/2/3 cup single (light) cream
Snipped chives, to garnish

Trim the leeks, cutting away most of the green. Slit the remainder and wash thoroughly. Slice thickly. Place in a 2 litre/3½ pt/8½ cup dish with the potatoes, butter or margarine and water. Cover with a plate and cook on Full for 12 minutes, stirring four times. Transfer to a blender, add the milk and work to a purée. Return to the dish. Mix the cornflour smoothly with the water and add to the dish. Season to taste with the salt. Cook, uncovered, on Full for 6 minutes, beating every minute. Allow to cool. Stir in the cream. Cover and chill thoroughly. Ladle into bowls and sprinkle each serving with chives.

Chilled Cucumber Soup with Yoghurt

Serves 6–8

25 g/1 oz/2 tbsp butter or margarine
1 large garlic clove
1 cucumber, peeled and coarsely grated
600 ml/1 pt/2½ cups plain yoghurt
300 ml/½ pt/1¼ cups milk
150 ml/¼ pt/2/3 cup cold water
2.5–10 ml/½–2 tsp salt
Chopped mint, to garnish

Place the butter or margarine in a 1.75 litre/3 pt/7½ cup dish. Heat, uncovered, on Full for 1 minute. Crush in the garlic and add the cucumber. Cook, uncovered, on Full for 4 minutes, stirring twice. Remove from the microwave. Whisk in all the remaining ingredients. Cover and chill for several hours. Ladle into bowls and sprinkle each serving with mint.

Chilled Spinach Soup with Yoghurt

Serves 6–8

25 g/1 oz/2 tbsp butter or margarine
1 large garlic clove
450 g/1 lb young spinach leaves, shredded
600 ml/1 pt/2½ cups plain yoghurt
300 ml/½ pt/1¼ cups milk
150 ml/¼ pt/2/3 cup cold water
2.5–10 ml/½–2 tsp salt
Juice of 1 lemon
Grated nutmeg or ground walnuts, to garnish

Place the butter or margarine in a 1.75 litre/3 pt/7½ cup dish. Heat, uncovered, on Full for 1 minute. Crush in the garlic and add the spinach. Cook, uncovered, on Full for 4 minutes, stirring twice. Remove from the microwave. Blend to a coarse purée in a blender or food processor. Whisk in all the remaining ingredients. Cover and chill for several hours. Ladle into bowls and dust each serving with nutmeg or ground walnuts.

Sherried Chilled Tomato Soup

Serves 4–5

300 ml/½ pt/1¼ cups water
300 ml/10 fl oz/1 can condensed tomato soup
30 ml/2 tbsp dry sherry
150 ml/¼ pt/2/3 cup double (heavy) cream
5 ml/1 tsp Worcestershire sauce
Snipped chives, to garnish

Pour the water into a 1.25 litre/ 2¼ pt/5½ cup bowl and heat, uncovered, on Full for 4–5 minutes until it just begins to bubble. Whisk in the tomato soup. When completely smooth, thoroughly stir in the remaining ingredients. Cover and chill for 4–5 hours. Stir round, ladle into glass dishes and sprinkle each with chives.

New England Fish Chowder

Serves 6–8

Always served in North America for Sunday brunch, Clam Chowder is the ultimate classic but, as clams are not that easy to come by, white fish has been substituted.

5 streaky bacon rashers (slices), coarsely chopped
1 large onion, peeled and grated
15 ml/1 tbsp cornflour (cornstarch)
30 ml/2 tbsp cold water
450 g/1 lb potatoes, cut into 1 cm/½ in cubes
900 ml/1½ pts/3¾ cups hot full-cream milk
450 g/1lb firm white fish fillets, skinned and cut into bite-sized pieces
2.5 ml/½ tsp ground nutmeg
Salt and freshly ground black pepper

Place the bacon in a 2.5 litre/4½ pt/ 11 cup bowl. Add the onion and cook, uncovered, on Full for 5 minutes. Mix the cornflour smoothly with the water and stir into the bowl. Mix in the potatoes and half the hot milk. Cook, uncovered, on Full for 6 minutes, stirring three times. Mix in the remaining milk and cook, uncovered, on Full for 2 minutes. Add the fish with the nutmeg and season to taste. Cover with a plate and cook on Full for 2 minutes until the fish is tender. (Do not worry if the fish has begun to flake.) Ladle into deep bowls and eat straight away.

Crab Soup

Serves 4

25 g/1 oz/2 tbsp unsalted (sweet) butter
20 ml/4 tsp plain (all-purpose) flour
300 ml/½ pt/1¼ cups warmed full-cream milk
300 ml/½ pt/1¼ cups water
2.5 ml/½ tsp English made mustard
A dash of hot pepper sauce
25 g/1 oz/¼ cup Cheddar cheese, grated
175 g/6 oz light and dark crabmeat
Salt and freshly ground black pepper
45 ml/3 tbsp dry sherry

Place the butter in a 1.75 litre/ 3 pt/7½ cup dish. Melt on Defrost for 1–1½ minutes. Stir in the flour. Cook, uncovered, on Full for 30 seconds. Gradually mix in the milk and water. Cook, uncovered, on Full for 5–6 minutes until smooth and thickened, beating every minute. Stir in all the remaining ingredients. Cook, uncovered, on Full for 1½–2 minutes, stirring twice, until hot.

Crab and Lemon Soup

Serves 4

Prepare as for Crab Soup, but add 5 ml/1 tsp finely grated lemon peel with the remaining ingredients. Dust each serving with a little grated nutmeg.

Lobster Bisque

Serves 4

Prepare as for Crab Soup, but substitute single (light) cream for the milk and chopped lobster meat for the crabmeat.

Dried Packet Soup

Tip the packet contents into a 1.25 litre/2¼ pt/5½ cup dish. Gradually stir in the recommended amount of cold water. Cover and allow to stand for 20 minutes to soften the vegetables. Stir. Cover with a plate and cook on Full for 6–8 minutes, stirring twice, until the soup comes to the boil and thickens. Allow to stand for 3 minutes. Stir round and serve.

Canned Condensed Soup

Tip the soup into a 1.25 litre/2¼ pt/ 5½ cup measuring jug. Add 1 can of boiling water and whisk thoroughly. Cover with a plate or saucer and heat on Full for 6–7 minutes, whisking twice, until the soup just comes to the boil. Pour into bowls and serve.

Reheating Soups

For successful results, reheat clear or thin soups on Full and creamy soups and broths on Defrost.

Warming Eggs for Cooking

Invaluable if you decide at the last minute to do some baking and need eggs at room temperature.

For 1 egg: break the egg into a small dish or cup. Puncture the yolk twice with a skewer or the tip of a knife to prevent the skin bursting and yolk exploding. Cover the dish or cup with a saucer. Warm on Defrost for 30 seconds.

For 2 eggs: as for 1 egg but warm for 30–45 seconds.

For 3 eggs: as for 1 egg but warm for 1–1¼ minutes.

Poached Eggs

These are best cooked individually in their own dishes.

For 1 egg: pour 90 ml/6 tbsp hot water into a shallow dish. Add 2.5 ml/½ tsp mild vinegar to prevent the white spreading. Carefully slide in 1 egg, first broken into a cup. Puncture the yolk twice with a skewer or the tip of a knife. Cover with a plate and cook on Full for 45 seconds–1¼ minutes, depending on how firm you like the whites. Allow to stand for 1 minute. Lift out of the dish with a perforated fish slice.

For 2 eggs cooked in 2 dishes simultaneously: cook on Full for 1½ minutes. Allow to stand for 1¼ minutes. If the whites are too runny, cook for a further 15–20 seconds.

For 3 eggs cooked in 3 dishes simultaneously: cook on Full for 2–2½ minutes. Allow to stand for 2 minutes. If the whites are too runny, cook for a further 20–30 seconds.

Fried (Sautéed) Eggs

The microwave does a superb job here and the eggs turn out soft and tender, always sunny-side up and with a fringe of white that never frizzles. Frying more than 2 eggs at a time is not recommended as the yolks would cook more quickly than the whites and become hard. This is due to the longer cooking time needed to set the whites. Use china or pottery without any hint of decoration, as they do in France.

For 1 egg: brush a small china or pottery dish lightly with melted butter, margarine or a trace of delicate olive oil. Break the egg into a cup, then slide it into the prepared dish. Puncture the yolk twice with a skewer or the tip of a knife. Sprinkle lightly with salt and freshly ground black pepper. Cover with a plate and cook on Full for 30 seconds. Allow to stand for 1 minute. Continue to cook for a further 15–20 seconds. If the white is not sufficiently set cook for a further 5–10 seconds.

For 2 eggs: as for 1 egg, but cook on Full for 1 minute initially, then stand for 1 minute. Cook for a further 20–40 seconds. If the whites are not sufficiently set, allow a further 6–8 seconds.

Piperade

Serves 4

30 ml/2 tbsp olive oil
3 onions, very thinly sliced
2 green (bell) peppers, seeded and finely chopped
6 tomatoes, blanched, skinned, seeded, and chopped
15 ml/1 tbsp chopped basil leaves
Salt and freshly ground black pepper
6 large eggs
60 ml/4 tbsp double (heavy) cream
Toast, to serve

Pour the oil into a deep 25 cm/10 in diameter dish and heat, uncovered, on Full for 1 minute. Stir in the onions and peppers. Cover with a plate and cook on Defrost for 12–14 minutes until the vegetables are tender. Stir in the tomatoes and basil and season to taste. Cover as before and cook on Full for 3 minutes. Thoroughly beat together the eggs and cream and season to taste. Pour into the dish and combine with the vegetables. Cook, uncovered, on Full for 4–5 minutes until lightly scrambled, stirring every minute. Cover and allow to stand for 3 minutes before serving with crisp toast.

Piperade with Gammon

Serves 4

Prepare as for Piperade but serve spooned on portions of fried (sautéed) bread and top each with a grilled (broiled) or microwaved gammon rasher (slice).

Piperada

Serves 4

Spain's version of Piperade.

Prepare as for Piperade, but add 2 garlic cloves, crushed, with the onions and green (bell) peppers and add 125 g/4 oz/1 cup coarsely chopped ham to the cooked vegetables. Garnish each portion with sliced stuffed olives.

Eggs Florentine

Serves 4

450 g/1lb freshly cooked spinach
60 ml/4 tbsp whipping cream
4 poached eggs, cooked 2 at a time
300 ml/½ pt/1¼ cups hot Cheese Sauce or Mornay Sauce
50 g/2 oz/½ cup grated cheese

Work together the spinach and cream in a food processor or blender. Arrange in a buttered shallow heatproof 18 cm/7 in diameter dish. Cover with a plate and heat on Full for 1½ minutes. Arrange the eggs on top and coat with the hot sauce. Sprinkle with the cheese and brown under a hot grill (broiler).

Poached Egg Rossini

SERVES 1

This makes for an elegant light lunch with a leafy side salad.

Fry (sauté) or toast de-crusted slices of wheatmeal bread. Spread with a smooth liver pâté containing, if cost permits, some truffle. Top with a freshly cooked poached egg and serve immediately.

Aubergine Egg Scramble

Serves 4

An Israeli idea that converts well to the microwave. The flavour is curiously powerful.

750 g/1½ lb aubergines (eggplants)
15 ml/1 tbsp lemon juice
15 ml/1 tbsp corn or sunflower oil
2 onions, finely chopped
2 garlic cloves, crushed
4 large eggs
60 ml/4 tbsp milk
Salt and freshly ground black pepper
Hot buttered toast, to serve

Top and tail the aubergines and halve them lengthways. Arrange on a large plate, cut sides down, and cover with kitchen paper. Cook on

Full for 8–9 minutes or until soft. Scoop the flesh out of the skins directly into a food processor with the lemon juice and work to a coarse purée. Place the oil in a 1.5 litre/2½ pt/6 cup dish. Heat, uncovered, on Full for 30 seconds. Stir in the onions and garlic. Cook, uncovered, on Full for 5 minutes. Beat the eggs with the milk and season thoroughly to taste. Pour into the dish and scramble with the onions and garlic on Full for 2 minutes, stirring every 30 seconds. Mix in the onions and garlic and add the aubergine purée. Continue to cook, uncovered, on Full for 3–4 minutes, stirring every 30 seconds, until the mixture thickens and the eggs are scrambled. Serve on hot buttered toast.

Classic Omelette

Serves 1

A light-textured omelette that can be served plain or filled.

Melted butter or margarine

3 eggs

20 ml/4 tsp salt

Freshly ground black pepper

30 ml/2 tbsp cold water

Parsley or watercress, to garnish

Brush a shallow 20 cm/8 in diameter dish with melted butter or margarine. Beat the eggs very thoroughly with all the remaining ingredients except the garnish. (Lightly breaking up the eggs, as for traditional omelettes, is not enough.) Pour into the dish, cover with a plate and transfer to the microwave. Cook on Full for 1½ minutes. Uncover and stir the egg mixture gently with a wooden spoon or fork, bringing the partially set edges to the centre. Cover as before and return to the microwave. Cook on Full for 1½ minutes. Uncover and continue to cook for 30–60 seconds or until the top is just set. Fold into three and slide out on to a warmed plate. Garnish and serve immediately.

Flavoured Omelettes

Serves 1

Parsley Omelette: prepare as for Classic Omelette, but sprinkle the eggs with 30 ml/2 tbsp chopped parsley after the omelette has cooked for the initial 1½ minutes.

Chive Omelette: prepare as for Classic Omelette, but sprinkle the eggs with 30 ml/2 tbsp snipped chives after the omelette has cooked for the initial 1½ minutes.

Watercress Omelette: prepare as for Classic Omelette, but sprinkle the eggs with 30 ml/2 tbsp chopped watercress after the omelette has cooked for the initial 1½ minutes.

Omelette aux Fines Herbes: prepare as for Classic Omelette, but sprinkle the eggs with 45 ml/3 tbsp mixed chopped parsley, chervil and basil after the omelette has cooked for the initial 1½ minutes. A little fresh tarragon may also be added.

Curried Omelette with Coriander: prepare as for Classic Omelette, but beat the eggs and water with 5–10 ml/1–2 tsp curry powder in addition to the salt and pepper. Sprinkle the eggs with 30 ml/2 tbsp chopped coriander (cilantro) after the omelette has cooked for the initial 1½ minutes.

Cheese and Mustard Omelette: prepare as for Classic Omelette, but beat the eggs and water with 5 ml/1 tsp made mustard and 30 ml/2 tbsp very finely grated and well-flavoured hard cheese in addition to the salt and pepper.

Brunch Omelette

Serves 1–2

A North American-style omelette, traditionally served at Sunday brunches. The Brunch Omelette may be flavoured and filled as for the Classic Omelette.

Prepare as for Classic Omelette, but substitute 45 ml/3 tbsp cold milk for the 30 ml/2 tbsp water. After uncovering, cook on Full for 1–1½ minutes. Fold into three and carefully slide on to a plate.

Poached Egg with Melted Cheese

Serves 1

1 slice hot buttered toast
45 ml/3 tbsp cream cheese
Tomato ketchup (catsup)
1 poached egg
60–75 ml/4–5 tbsp grated cheese
Paprika

Spread the toast with the cream cheese, then with tomato ketchup. Place on a plate. Top with the poached egg, then shower with the grated cheese and dust with paprika. Heat, uncovered, on Defrost for 1–1½ minutes until the cheese is just beginning to melt. Eat straight away.

Eggs Benedict

Serves 1–2

No North American Sunday brunch would be complete without Eggs Benedict, a wickedly rich egg concoction that defies all calorie and cholesterol restrictions.

Split and toast a muffin or bap. Top with a rasher (slice) of conventionally grilled (broiled) mild bacon, then top both halves with a freshly poached egg. Coat with Hollandaise Sauce, then dust lightly with paprika. Eat straight away.

Omelette Arnold Bennett

Serves 2

Said to have been created by a chef at London's Savoy Hotel in honour of the famous writer, this is a monumental and memorable omelette for every high day and feast day.

175 g/6 oz smoked haddock or cod fillet
45 ml/3 tbsp boiling water
120 ml/4 fl oz/½ cup crème fraîche
Freshly ground black pepper
Melted butter or margarine, for brushing
3 eggs
45 ml/3 tbsp cold milk
A pinch of salt
50 g/2 oz/½ cup coloured Cheddar or Red Leicester cheese, grated

Place the fish in a shallow dish with the water. Cover with a plate and cook on Full for 5 minutes. Allow to stand for 2 minutes. Drain and flake up the flesh with a fork. Work in the crème fraîche and season to taste with pepper. Brush a 20 cm/8 in diameter shallow dish with melted butter or margarine. Beat the eggs thoroughly with the milk and salt. Pour into the dish. Cover with a plate and cook on Full for 3 minutes, moving the setting edges into the centre half-way through cooking. Uncover and cook on Full for a further 30 seconds. Spread with the fish and cream mixture and sprinkle with the cheese. Cook, uncovered, on Full for 1–1½ minutes until the omelette is hot and the cheese has melted. Divide into two servings and serve straight away.

Tortilla

Serves 2

The renowned Spanish Omelette is round and flat as a pancake. It teams comfortably with chunks of bread or rolls and a crisp green salad.

15 ml/1 tbsp butter, margarine or olive oil
1 onion, finely chopped
175 g/6 oz cooked potatoes, diced
3 eggs
5 ml/1 tsp salt
30 ml/2 tbsp cold water

Put the butter, margarine or oil in a deep 20 cm/8 in diameter dish. Heat on Defrost for 30–45 seconds. Mix in the onion. Cover with a plate and cook on Defrost for 2 minutes. Stir in the potatoes. Cover as before and cook on Full for 1 minute. Remove from the microwave. Beat the eggs thoroughly with the salt and water. Pour evenly over the onions and potatoes. Cook, uncovered, on Full for 4½ minutes, turning the dish once. Allow to stand for 1 minute, then divide into two and transfer each portion to a plate. Eat straight away.

Spanish Omelette with Mixed Vegetables

Serves 2

30 ml/2 tbsp butter, margarine or olive oil

1 onion, finely chopped

2 tomatoes, skinned and chopped

½ small green or red (bell) pepper, finely chopped

3 eggs

5–7.5 ml/1–1½ tsp salt

30 ml/2 tbsp cold water

Put the butter, margarine or oil in a deep 20 cm/8 in diameter dish. Heat on Defrost for 1½ minutes. Mix in the onion, tomatoes and chopped pepper. Cover with a plate and cook on Defrost for 6–7 minutes until tender. Beat the eggs thoroughly with the salt and water. Pour evenly over the vegetables. Cover with a plate and cook on Full for 5–6 minutes until the eggs are set, turning the dish once. Divide into two and transfer each portion to a plate. Eat straight away.

Spanish Omelette with Ham

Serves 2

Prepare as for Spanish Omelette with Mixed Vegetables, but add 60 ml/4 tbsp coarsely chopped air-dried Spanish ham and 1–2 garlic cloves, crushed, to the vegetables and cook for 30 seconds longer.

Cheesy Eggs in Celery Sauce

Serves 4

A short-cut lunch or supper dish, providing an ample meal for vegetarians.

6 large hard-boiled (hard-cooked) eggs, shelled and halved
300 ml/10 fl oz/1 can condensed celery soup
45 ml/3 tbsp full-cream milk
175 g/6 oz/1½ cups Cheddar cheese, grated
30 ml/2 tbsp finely chopped parsley
Salt and freshly ground black pepper
15 ml/1 tbsp toasted breadcrumbs
2.5 ml/½ tsp paprika

Arrange the egg halves in a deep 20 cm/8 in diameter dish. In a separate bowl or dish, gently mix together the soup and milk. Heat, uncovered, on Full for 4 minutes, whisking every minute. Mix in half the cheese and heat, uncovered, on Full for 1–1½ minutes until melted. Stir in the parsley, season to taste, then spoon over the eggs. Sprinkle with the remaining cheese, the breadcrumbs and paprika. Brown under a hot grill (broiler) before serving.

Eggs Fu Yung

Serves 2

5 ml/1 tbsp butter, margarine or corn oil
1 onion, finely chopped
30 ml/2 tbsp cooked peas
30 ml/2 tbsp cooked or canned bean sprouts
125 g/4 oz mushrooms, sliced
3 large eggs
2.5 ml/½ tsp salt
30 ml/2 tbsp cold water
5 ml/1 tsp soy sauce
4 spring onions (scallions), finely sliced

Put the butter, margarine or oil in a deep 20 cm/8 in diameter dish and heat, uncovered, on Defrost for 1 minute. Mix in the chopped onion, cover with a plate and cook on Full for 2 minutes. Stir in the peas, bean sprouts and mushrooms. Cover as before and cook on Full for 1½ minutes. Remove from the microwave and stir. Beat the eggs thoroughly with the salt, water and soy sauce. Pour evenly over the vegetables. Cook, uncovered, on Full for 5 minutes, turning twice. Allow to stand for 1 minute. Divide into two and transfer each to a warmed plate. Garnish with the spring onions and serve straight away.

Pizza Omelette

Serves 2

A novelty pizza, the base made from a flat omelette instead of yeast dough.

15 ml/1 tbsp olive oil
3 large eggs
45 ml/3 tbsp milk
2.5 ml/½ tsp salt
4 tomatoes, blanched, skinned and sliced
125 g/4 oz/1 cup Mozzarella cheese, grated
8 canned anchovies in oil
8–12 stoned (pitted) black olives

Put the oil in a deep 20 cm/8 in diameter dish and heat, uncovered, on Defrost for 1 minutes. Beat the eggs very thoroughly with the milk and salt. Pour into the dish and cover with a plate. Cook on Full for 3 minutes, moving the setting edges to the centre of the dish half-way through cooking. Uncover and cook on Full for a further 30 seconds. Spread with the tomatoes and cheese, then garnish with the anchovies and olives. Cook, uncovered, on Full for 4 minutes, turning twice. Divide into two and serve straight away.

Soufflé Omelette

Serves 2

45 ml/3 tbsp jam (conserve)
Icing (confectioners') sugar
Melted butter
3 drops lemon juice
3 large eggs, separated
15 ml/1 tbsp caster (superfine) sugar

Spoon the jam into a small dish or cup. Cover with a saucer and heat on Defrost for 1½ minutes. Carefully remove from the microwave, leave covered and set aside. Cover a large sheet of greaseproof (waxed) paper with sifted icing sugar. Brush a deep 25 cm/10 in diameter dish with melted butter. Add the lemon juice to the egg whites and beat until stiffly peaking. Add the caster sugar to the egg yolks and beat until thick, pale and creamy. Gently whisk the beaten whites into the yolks until smooth and evenly combined. Spoon into the prepared dish. Cook, uncovered, on Full for 3½ minutes. Invert on to the sugared paper, score a line down the centre with a knife and spread the warm jam over half the omelette. Gently fold in half, cut into two portions and eat straight away.

Lemon Soufflé Omelette

Serves 2

Prepare as for Soufflé Omelette, but add 5 ml/1 tsp finely grated lemon rind to the beaten egg yolks and sugar.

Orange Soufflé Omelette

Serves 2

Prepare as for Soufflé Omelette, but add 5 ml/1 tsp finely grated orange rind to the beaten egg yolks and sugar.

Almond and Apricot Soufflé Omelette

Serves 2

Prepare as for Soufflé Omelette, but add 2.5 ml/½ tsp almond essence (extract) to the beaten egg yolks and sugar. Fill with warmed smooth apricot jam (conserve).

Raspberry Soufflé Omelette

Serves 2

Prepare as for Soufflé Omelette, but add 2.5 ml/½ tsp vanilla essence (extract) to the beaten egg yolks and sugar. Fill with 45–60 ml/3–4 tbsp coarsely crushed raspberries mixed with icing (confectioners') sugar to taste and a dash of Kirsch or gin.

Strawberry Soufflé Omelette

Serves 2

Prepare as for Soufflé Omelette, but add 2.5 ml/½ tsp vanilla essence (extract) to the beaten egg yolks and sugar. Fill with 45–60 ml/3–4 tbsp thinly sliced strawberries mixed with icing (confectioners') sugar to taste and 15 ml/1 tbsp chocolate or orange liqueur.

Soufflé Omelette with Toppings

Serves 2

Prepare as for Soufflé Omelette, but instead of folding and cutting the omelette into halves, leave flat and cut into two portions. Transfer each to a plate and top with either warmed stewed fruit or a fruit coulis. Serve straight away.

Baked Egg with Cream

Serves 1

This way of preparing eggs is highly esteemed in France, where it is called oeufs en cocotte. It is certainly a top-drawer starter for dinner parties but it also makes a stylish lunch with toast or crackers and a green salad. To ensure success, it is advisable to cook one egg at a time in an individual dish.

1 egg

Salt and freshly ground black pepper
15 ml/1 tbsp double (heavy) cream or crème fraîche
5 ml/1 tsp very finely chopped parsley, chives or coriander (cilantro)

Brush a small ramekin dish (custard cup) or individual soufflé dish with melted butter or margarine. Gently break in the egg and puncture the yolk twice with a skewer or the tip of a knife. Season well to taste. Coat with the cream and sprinkle with the herbs. Cover with a saucer and cook on Defrost for 3 minutes. Allow to stand for 1 minute before eating.

Baked Egg Neapolitan

Serves 1

Prepare as for Baked Egg with Cream, but coat the egg with 15 ml/1 tbsp passata (sieved tomatoes) and two finely chopped black olives or capers.

Cheese Fondue

Serves 6

Born in Switzerland, Cheese Fondue is the après-ski darling of Alpine resorts or anywhere else with deep snow on high peaks. Dipping your bread into a communal pot of aromatic melted cheese is one of the most convivial, entertaining and relaxing ways of enjoying a meal with friends and there is no better kitchen helper for this than the microwave. Serve with small tots of Kirsch and cups of hot lemon tea for an authentic atmosphere.

1–2 garlic cloves, peeled and halved
175 g/6 oz/1½ cups Emmental cheese, grated
450 g/1 lb/4 cups Gruyère (Swiss) cheese, grated
15 ml/1 tbsp cornflour (cornstarch)
300 ml/½ pt/1¼ cups Mosel wine
5 ml/1 tsp lemon juice
30 ml/2 tbsp Kirsch
Salt and freshly ground black pepper
Cubed French bread, for dipping

Press the cut sides of the garlic halves against the sides of a deep 2.5 litre/4½ pt/11 cup glass or pottery dish. Alternatively, for a stronger taste, crush the garlic directly into the dish. Add both cheeses, the cornflour, wine and lemon juice. Cook, uncovered, on Full for 7–9 minutes, stirring four times, until the fondue begins to bubble gently.

Remove from the microwave and mix in the Kirsch. Season well to taste. Bring the dish to the table and eat by spearing a cube of bread on to a long fondue fork, swirling it round in the cheese mixture, then lifting it out.

Fondue with Cider

Serves 6

Prepare as for Cheese Fondue, but substitute dry cider for the wine and calvados for the Kirsch and serve cubes of red-skinned apple as well as the bread cubes for dipping.

Fondue with Apple Juice

Serves 6

A non-alcoholic Fondue with a mellow taste and suitable for all ages.

Prepare as for Cheese Fondue, but substitute apple juice for the wine and omit the Kirsch. If necessary, thin down with a little hot water.

Pink Fondue

Serves 6

Prepare as for Cheese Fondue, but substitute 200 g/7 oz/1¾ cups each white Cheshire cheese, Lancashire cheese and Caerphilly cheese for the Emmental and Gruyère (Swiss) cheeses and rosé wine for the white wine.

Smoky Fondue

Serves 6

Prepare as for Cheese Fondue, but substitute 200 g/7 oz/1¾ cups smoked cheese for half the Gruyère (Swiss) cheese. The quantity of Emmental cheese is unchanged.

German Beer Fondue

Serves 6

Prepare as for Cheese Fondue, but substitute beer for the wine and brandy for the Kirsch.

Fondue with Fire

Serves 6

Prepare as for Cheese Fondue, but add 2–3 red chillies, seeded and very finely chopped, just after the cornflour (cornstarch).

Curried Fondue

Serves 6

Prepare as for Cheese Fondue, but add 10–15 ml/2–3 tsp mild curry paste with the cheeses and substitute vodka for the Kirsch. Use pieces of warmed Indian bread for dipping.

Fonduta

Serves 4–6

An Italian version of Cheese Fondue, inordinately luscious.

Prepare as for Cheese Fondue, but substitute Italian Fontina cheese for the Gruyère (Swiss) and Emmental cheeses, dry white Italian wine for the Mosel, and marsala for the Kirsch.

Mock Cheese and Tomato Fondue

Serves 4–6

225 g/8 oz/2 cups mature Cheddar cheese, grated
125 g/4 oz/1 cup Lancashire or Wensleydale cheese, crumbled
300 ml/10 fl oz/1 can condensed tomato soup
10 ml/2 tsp Worcestershire sauce
A dash of hot pepper sauce
45 ml/3 tbsp dry sherry
Warmed ciabatta bread, to serve

Place all the ingredients except the sherry in a 1.25 litre/2¼ pt/5½ cup glass or pottery dish. Cook, uncovered, on Defrost for 7–9 minutes, stirring three or four times, until the fondue is smoothly thickened. Remove from the microwave and stir in the sherry. Eat with pieces of warm ciabatta bread.

Cheese Fondue

Serves 6

Born in Switzerland, Cheese Fondue is the après-ski darling of Alpine resorts or anywhere else with deep snow on high peaks. Dipping your bread into a communal pot of aromatic melted cheese is one of the most convivial, entertaining and relaxing ways of enjoying a meal with friends and there is no better kitchen helper for this than the microwave. Serve with small tots of Kirsch and cups of hot lemon tea for an authentic atmosphere.

1–2 garlic cloves, peeled and halved
175 g/6 oz/1½ cups Emmental cheese, grated
450 g/1 lb/4 cups Gruyère (Swiss) cheese, grated
15 ml/1 tbsp cornflour (cornstarch)
300 ml/½ pt/1¼ cups Mosel wine
5 ml/1 tsp lemon juice
30 ml/2 tbsp Kirsch
Salt and freshly ground black pepper
Cubed French bread, for dipping

Press the cut sides of the garlic halves against the sides of a deep 2.5 litre/4½ pt/11 cup glass or pottery dish. Alternatively, for a stronger taste, crush the garlic directly into the dish. Add both cheeses, the cornflour, wine and lemon juice. Cook, uncovered, on Full for 7–9 minutes, stirring four times, until the fondue begins to bubble gently.

Remove from the microwave and mix in the Kirsch. Season well to taste. Bring the dish to the table and eat by spearing a cube of bread on to a long fondue fork, swirling it round in the cheese mixture, then lifting it out.

Fondue with Cider

Serves 6

Prepare as for Cheese Fondue, but substitute dry cider for the wine and calvados for the Kirsch and serve cubes of red-skinned apple as well as the bread cubes for dipping.

Fondue with Apple Juice

Serves 6

A non-alcoholic Fondue with a mellow taste and suitable for all ages.

Prepare as for Cheese Fondue, but substitute apple juice for the wine and omit the Kirsch. If necessary, thin down with a little hot water.

Pink Fondue

Serves 6

Prepare as for Cheese Fondue, but substitute 200 g/7 oz/1¾ cups each white Cheshire cheese, Lancashire cheese and Caerphilly cheese for the Emmental and Gruyère (Swiss) cheeses and rosé wine for the white wine.

Smoky Fondue

Serves 6

Prepare as for Cheese Fondue, but substitute 200 g/7 oz/1¾ cups smoked cheese for half the Gruyère (Swiss) cheese. The quantity of Emmental cheese is unchanged.

German Beer Fondue

Serves 6

Prepare as for Cheese Fondue, but substitute beer for the wine and brandy for the Kirsch.

Fondue with Fire

Serves 6

Prepare as for Cheese Fondue, but add 2–3 red chillies, seeded and very finely chopped, just after the cornflour (cornstarch).

Curried Fondue

Serves 6

Prepare as for Cheese Fondue, but add 10–15 ml/2–3 tsp mild curry paste with the cheeses and substitute vodka for the Kirsch. Use pieces of warmed Indian bread for dipping.

Fonduta

Serves 4–6

An Italian version of Cheese Fondue, inordinately luscious.

Prepare as for Cheese Fondue, but substitute Italian Fontina cheese for the Gruyère (Swiss) and Emmental cheeses, dry white Italian wine for the Mosel, and marsala for the Kirsch.

Mock Cheese and Tomato Fondue

Serves 4–6

225 g/8 oz/2 cups mature Cheddar cheese, grated
125 g/4 oz/1 cup Lancashire or Wensleydale cheese, crumbled
300 ml/10 fl oz/1 can condensed tomato soup
10 ml/2 tsp Worcestershire sauce
A dash of hot pepper sauce
45 ml/3 tbsp dry sherry
Warmed ciabatta bread, to serve

Place all the ingredients except the sherry in a 1.25 litre/2¼ pt/5½ cup glass or pottery dish. Cook, uncovered, on Defrost for 7–9 minutes, stirring three or four times, until the fondue is smoothly thickened. Remove from the microwave and stir in the sherry. Eat with pieces of warm ciabatta bread.

Mock Cheese and Celery Fondue

Serves 4–6

Prepare as for Mock Cheese and Tomato Fondue, but substitute condensed celery soup for the tomato soup and flavour with gin instead of sherry.

Italian Cheese, Cream and Egg Fondue

Serves 4–6

1 garlic clove, crushed
50 g/2 oz/¼ cup unsalted (sweet) butter, at kitchen temperature
450 g/1 lb/4 cups Fontina cheese, grated
60 ml/4 tbsp cornflour (cornstarch)
300 ml/½ pt/1¼ cups milk
2.5 ml/½ tsp grated nutmeg
Salt and freshly ground black pepper
150 ml/¼ pt/2/3 cup whipping cream
2 eggs, beaten
Cubed Italian bread, to serve

Place the garlic, butter, cheese, cornflour, milk and nutmeg in a deep 2.5 litre/4½ pt/11 cup glass or pottery dish. Season to taste. Cook, uncovered, on Full for 7–9 minutes, stirring four times, until the fondue begins to bubble gently. Remove from the microwave and mix in the cream. Cook, uncovered, on Full for 1 minute. Remove from the microwave and gradually beat in the eggs. Serve with Italian bread for dipping.

Dutch Farmhouse Fondue

Serves 4–6

A soft and gentle fondue, mild enough for children.

1 garlic clove, crushed
15 ml/1 tbsp butter
450 g/1 lb/4 cups Gouda cheese, grated
15 ml/1 tbsp cornflour (cornstarch)
20 ml/4 tsp mustard powder
A pinch of grated nutmeg
300 ml/½ pt/1¼ cup full-cream milk
Salt and freshly ground black pepper
Cubed bread, to serve

Place all the ingredients in a deep 2.5 litre/4½ pt/11 cup glass or pottery dish, seasoning well to taste. Cook, uncovered, on Full for 7–9 minutes, stirring four times, until the fondue begins to bubble gently. Bring the dish to the table and eat by spearing a cube of bread on to a long fondue fork, swirling it round in the cheese mixture, then lifting it out.

Farmhouse Fondue with a Kick

Serves 4–6

Prepare as for Dutch Farmhouse Fondue, but stir in 30–45 ml/2–3 tbsp Genever (Dutch gin) after cooking.

Baked Egg Flamenco Style

Serves 1

Melted butter or margarine
1 small tomato, blanched, skinned and chopped
2 spring onions (scallions), chopped
1–2 stuffed olives, sliced
5 ml/1 tsp oil
15 ml/1 tbsp cooked ham, finely chopped
1 egg
Salt and freshly ground black pepper
15 ml/1 tbsp double (heavy) cream or crème fraîche
5 ml/1 tsp very finely chopped parsley, chives or coriander (cilantro)

Brush a small ramekin dish (custard cup) or individual soufflé dish with melted butter or margarine. Add the tomato, spring onions, olives, oil and ham. Cover with a saucer and heat through on Full for 1 minute. Gently break in the egg and puncture the yolk twice with a skewer or the tip of a knife. Season well to taste. Coat with the cream and sprinkle with the herbs. Cover as before and cook on Defrost for 3 minutes. Allow to stand for 1 minute before eating.

Bread and Butter Cheese and Parsley Pudding

Serves 4–6

4 large slices white bread
50 g/2 oz/¼ cup butter, at kitchen temperature
175 g/6 oz/1½ cups orange-coloured Cheddar cheese
45 ml/3 tbsp chopped parsley
600 ml/1 pt/2½ cups cold milk
3 eggs
5 ml/1 tsp salt
Paprika

Spread the bread with the butter and cut each slice into four squares. Thoroughly butter a 1.75 litre/3 pt/7½ cup dish. Arrange half the bread squares, buttered sides up, over the base of the dish. Sprinkle with two-thirds of the cheese and all the parsley. Arrange the remaining bread on top, buttered sides up. Pour the milk into a jug and warm, uncovered, on Full for 3 minutes. Beat the eggs until foamy, then gradually whisk in the milk. Stir in the salt. Pour gently over the bread and butter. Sprinkle the remaining cheese on top and dust with paprika. Cover with kitchen paper and cook on Defrost for 30 minutes. Allow to stand for 5 minutes, then brown under a hot grill (broiler), if liked, before serving.

Bread and Butter Cheese and Parsley Pudding with Cashew Nuts

Serves 4–6

Prepare as for Bread and Butter Cheese and Parsley Pudding, but add 45 ml/3 tbsp cashew nuts, toasted and coarsely chopped, with the cheese and parsley.

Four-cheese Bread and Butter Pudding

Serves 4–6

Prepare as for Bread and Butter Cheese and Parsley Pudding, but use a mixture of grated Cheddar, Edam, Red Leicester and crumbled Stilton cheeses. Substitute four chopped pickled onions for the parsley.

Cheese and Egg Crumpets

Serves 4

300 ml/10 fl oz/1 can condensed mushroom soup
45 ml/3 tbsp single (light) cream
125 g/4 oz/1 cup Red Leicester cheese, grated
4 hot toasted crumpets
4 freshly poached eggs

Put the soup, cream and half the cheese into a 900 ml/1½ pt/3¾ cup bowl. Heat, uncovered, on Full for 4–5 minutes until hot and smooth, beating every minute. Put each crumpet on a warmed plate and top with an egg. Coat with the mushroom mixture, sprinkle with the remaining cheese and heat one at a time on Full for about 1 minute until the cheese is melted and bubbling. Eat straight away.

Upside-down Cheese and Tomato Pudding

Serves 4

225 g/8 oz/2 cups self-raising (self-rising) flour
5 ml/1 tsp mustard powder
5 ml/1 tsp salt
125 g/4 oz/½ cup butter or margarine
125 g/4 oz/1 cup Edam or Cheddar cheese, grated
2 eggs, beaten
150 ml/¼ pt/2/3 cup cold milk
4 large tomatoes, blanched and skinned and chopped
15 ml/1 tbsp chopped parsley or coriander (cilantro)

Grease a deep round 1.75 litre/3 pt/7½ cup pudding basin with butter. Sift the flour, mustard powder and 2.5 ml/½ tsp of the salt into a bowl. Rub in the butter or margarine finely, then toss in the cheese. Mix to a soft consistency with the eggs and milk. Spread smoothly into the prepared basin. Cook, uncovered, on Full for 6 minutes. Mix the tomatoes with the remaining salt. Place in a shallow bowl and cover with a plate. Remove the pudding from the oven and carefully invert into a shallow dish. Cover with kitchen paper and cook on Full for a further 2 minutes. Remove from the oven and cover with a piece of foil to retain the heat. Put the tomatoes in the microwave and heat on Full for 3 minutes. Spoon over the pudding, sprinkle with the herbs and serve hot.

Pizza Crumpets

Serves 4

45 ml/3 tbsp tomato purée (paste)
30 ml/2 tbsp olive oil
1 garlic clove, crushed
4 hot toasted crumpets
2 tomatoes, thinly sliced
175 g/6 oz Mozzarella cheese, sliced
12 black olives

Mix together the tomato purée, olive oil and garlic and spread on to the crumpets. Arrange the tomato slices on top. Cover with the cheese and stud with the olives. Heat one at a time on Full for about 1–1½ minutes until the cheese is starting to melt. Eat straight away.

Gingered Sea Bass with Onions

Serves 8

A Cantonese speciality and a typical Chinese buffet dish.

2 sea bass, 450 g/1 lb each, cleaned but heads left on

8 spring onions (scallions)

5 ml/1 tsp salt

2.5 ml/½ tsp sugar

2.5 cm/1 in piece fresh root ginger, peeled and finely chopped

45 ml/3 tbsp soy sauce

Wash the fish inside and out. Dry with kitchen paper. Make three diagonal slashes with a sharp knife, about 2.5 cm/1 in apart, on both sides of each fish. Place head-to-tail in a 30 3 20 cm/12 3 8 in dish. Top and tail the onions, cut each into threads along its length and sprinkle over the fish. Thoroughly mix together the remaining ingredients and use to coat the fish. Cover the dish with clingfilm (plastic wrap) and slit it twice to allow steam to escape. Cook on Full for 12 minutes, turning the dish once. Transfer the fish to a serving plate and coat with the onions and juices from dish.

Trout Packets

Serves 2

Professional chefs call this truites en papillote. The parcels of simply prepared delicate trout make a smart fish course.

2 large cleaned trout, 450 g/1 lb each, washed but heads left on
1 onion, thickly sliced
1 small lemon or lime, thickly sliced
2 large dried bay leaves, coarsely crumbled
2.5 ml/½ tsp herbes de Provence
5 ml/1 tsp salt

Prepare two rectangles of baking parchment, 40 3 35 cm/16 3 14 in each. Place the onion and lemon or lime slices in the cavities of the fish with the bay leaves. Transfer to the parchment rectangles and sprinkle with the herbs and salt. Wrap each trout individually, then put both parcels together in a shallow dish. Cook on Full for 14 minutes, turning the dish once. Allow to stand for 2 minutes. Transfer each to a warmed plate and open out the parcels at the table.

Shining Monkfish with Slender Beans

Serves 4

125 g/4 oz French (green) or Kenya beans, topped and tailed

150 ml/¼ pt/2/3 cup boiling water

450 g/1 lb monkfish

15 ml/1 tbsp cornflour (cornstarch)

1.5–2.5 ml/¼–½ tsp Chinese five spice powder

45 ml/3 tbsp rice wine or medium sherry

5 ml/1 tsp bottled oyster sauce

2.5 ml/½ tsp sesame oil

1 garlic clove, crushed

50 ml/2 fl oz/3½ tbsp hot water

15 ml/1 tbsp soy sauce

Egg noodles, to serve

Halve the beans. Place in a round 1.25 litre/2¼ pt/5½ cup dish. Add the boiling water. Cover with clingfilm (plastic wrap) and slit it twice to allow steam to escape. Cook on Full for 4 minutes. Drain and set aside. Wash the monkfish and cut it into narrow strips. Mix the cornflour and spice powder with the rice wine or sherry until smooth. Stir in the remaining ingredients. Transfer to the dish in which the beans were cooked. Cook, uncovered, on Full for 1½ minutes. Stir until smooth, then mix in the beans and monkfish. Cover as before and cook on Full for 4 minutes. Allow to stand for 2 minutes, then stir round and serve.

Shining Prawns with Mangetout

Serves 4

Prepare as for Shining Monkfish with Slender Beans, but substitute mangetout (snow peas) for the beans and cook them for only 2½–3 minutes as they should remain crisp. Substitute shelled prawns (shrimp) for the monkfish.

Normandy Cod with Cider and Calvados

Serves 4

50 g/2 oz/¼ cup butter or margarine

1 onion, very thinly sliced

3 carrots, very thinly sliced

50 g/2 oz mushrooms, trimmed and thinly sliced

4 large cod steaks, about 225 g/8 oz each

5 ml/1 tsp salt

150 ml/¼ pt/2/3 cup cider

15 ml/1 tbsp cornflour (cornstarch)

25 ml/1½ tbsp cold water

15 ml/1 tbsp calvados

Parsley, to garnish

Place half the butter or margarine in a deep 20 cm/8 in diameter dish. Melt, uncovered, on Full for 45–60 seconds. Mix in the onion, carrots and mushrooms. Arrange the fish in a single layer on top. Dust with the salt. Pour the cider into the dish and dot the steaks with the remaining butter or margarine. Cover with clingfilm (plastic wrap) and slit it twice to allow steam to escape. Cook on Full for 8 minutes, turning the dish four times. Carefully pour off the cooking liquor and reserve. Mix the cornflour smoothly with the water and calvados. Add the fish juices. Cook, uncovered, on Full for 2–2½ minutes until the sauce thickens, whisking every 30 seconds. Arrange the fish on a warmed serving plate and top with the vegetables. Coat with the sauce and garnish with parsley.

Fish Paella

Serves 6–8

Spain's foremost rice dish, known worldwide through international travel.

900 g/2 lb skinned salmon fillet, cubed
1 packet saffron powder
60 ml/4 tbsp hot water
30 ml/2 tbsp olive oil
2 onions, chopped
2 garlic cloves, crushed
1 green (bell) pepper, seeded and coarsely chopped
225 g/8 oz/1 cup Italian or Spanish risotto rice
175 g/6 oz/1½ cups frozen or fresh peas
600 ml/1 pt/2½ cups boiling water
7.5 ml/1½ tsp salt
3 tomatoes, blanched, peeled and quartered
75 g/3 oz/¾ cup cooked ham, diced
125 g/4 oz/1 cup peeled prawns (shrimp)
250 g/9 oz/1 large can mussels in brine
Lemon wedges or slices, to garnish

Arrange the salmon cubes round the edge of a 25 cm/10 in diameter casserole dish (Dutch oven), leaving a small hollow in the centre. Cover the dish with clingfilm (plastic wrap) and slit it twice to allow steam to escape. Cook on Defrost for 10–11 minutes, turning the dish twice, until the fish looks flaky and just cooked. Drain off and reserve the liquid and set aside the salmon. Wash and dry the dish. Empty the saffron into a small bowl, add the hot water and leave to soak for 10 minutes. Pour the oil into the cleaned dish and add the onions, garlic and green pepper. Cook, uncovered, on Full for 4 minutes. Add the rice, saffron and soaking water, peas, salmon cubes, reserved salmon liquid, boiling water and salt. Mix thoroughly but gently. Cover as before and cook on Full for 10 minutes. Allow to stand in the microwave for 10 minutes. Cook on Full for a further 5 minutes. Uncover and carefully mix in the tomatoes and ham. Garnish with the prawns, mussels and lemon and serve.

Soused Herrings

Serves 4

4 herring, about 450 g/1 lb each, filleted
2 large bay leaves, coarsely crumbled
15 ml/1 tbsp mixed pickling spice
2 onions, sliced and separated into rings
150 ml/¼ pt/2/3 cup boiling water
20 ml/4 tsp granulated sugar
10 ml/2 tsp salt
90 ml/6 tbsp malt vinegar
Buttered bread, to serve

Roll up each herring fillet from the head to the tail end, skin sides inside. Arrange round the edge of a deep 25 cm/10 in diameter dish. Sprinkle with the bay leaves and spice. Arrange the onion rings between the herrings. Thoroughly mix together the remaining ingredients and spoon over the fish. Cover with clingfilm (plastic wrap) and slit it twice to allow steam to escape. Cook on Full for 18 minutes. Allow to cool, then chill. Eat cold with bread and butter.

Moules Marinières

Serves 4

Belgium's national dish, always served with a side dish of chips (fries).

900 ml/2 pts/5 cups fresh mussels

15 g/½ oz/1 tbsp butter or margarine

1 small onion, chopped

1 garlic clove, crushed

150 ml/¼ pt/2/3 cup dry white wine

1 bouquet garni sachet

1 dried bay leaf, crumbled

7.5 ml/1½ tsp salt

20 ml/4 tsp fresh white breadcrumbs

20 ml/4 tsp chopped parsley

Wash the mussels under cold running water. Scrape away any barnacles, then cut off the beards. Discard any mussels with cracked shells or those that are open; they can cause food poisoning. Wash again. Put the butter or margarine in a deep bowl. Melt, uncovered, on Full for about 30 seconds. Mix in the onion and garlic. Cover with a plate and cook on Full for 6 minutes, stirring twice. Add the wine, bouquet garni, bay leaf, salt and mussels. Stir gently to mix. Cover as before and cook on Full for 5 minutes. Using a slotted spoon, transfer the mussels into four deep bowls or soup plates. Stir the breadcrumbs and half the parsley into the cooking liquid, then spoon over the mussels. Sprinkle with the remaining parsley and serve straight away.

Mackerel with Rhubarb and Raisin Sauce

Serves 4

The prettily coloured sweet-sour sauce balances the rich mackerel beautifully.

350 g/12 oz young rhubarb, coarsely chopped
60 ml/4 tbsp boiling water
30 ml/2 tbsp raisins
30 ml/2 tbsp granulated sugar
2.5 ml/½ tsp vanilla essence (extract)
Finely grated zest and juice of ½ small lemon
4 mackerel, cleaned, boned and heads discarded
50 g/2 oz/¼ cup butter or margarine
Salt and freshly ground black pepper

Place the rhubarb and water in a casserole dish (Dutch oven). Cover with clingfilm (plastic wrap) and slit it twice to allow steam to escape. Cook on Full for 6 minutes, turning the dish three times. Uncover and mash the rhubarb to a pulp. Stir in the raisins, sugar, vanilla essence and lemon zest, then set aside. With the skin sides facing you, fold each mackerel in half crossways from head to tail. Put the butter or margarine and lemon juice in a deep 20 cm/8 in diameter dish. Melt on Full for 2 minutes. Add the fish and coat with the melted ingredients. Sprinkle with salt and pepper. Cover with clingfilm (plastic wrap) and slit it twice to allow steam to escape. Cook on Medium for 14–16 minutes until the fish looks flaky. Allow to stand for 2 minutes. Heat through the rhubarb sauce on Full for 1 minute and serve with the mackerel.

Herring with Apple Cider Sauce

Serves 4

Prepare as for Mackerel with Rhubarb and Raisin Sauce, but substitute peeled and cored cooking (tart) apples for the rhubarb and boiling cider in place of the water. Omit the raisins.

Carp in Jellied Sauce

Serves 4

1 very fresh carp, cleaned and cut into 8 thin slices
30 ml/2 tbsp malt vinegar
3 carrots, thinly sliced
3 onions, thinly sliced
600 ml/1 pt/2½ cups boiling water
10–15 ml/2–3 tsp salt

Wash the carp, then soak for 3 hours in enough cold water with the vinegar added to cover the fish. (This removes the muddy taste.) Place the carrots and onions in a deep 23 cm/9 in diameter dish with the boiling water and salt. Cover with clingfilm (plastic wrap) and slit it twice to allow steam to escape. Cook on Full for 20 minutes, turning the dish four times. Drain, reserving the liquid. (The vegetables can be used elsewhere in fish soup or stir-fries.) Pour the liquid back into the dish. Add the carp in a single layer. Cover as before and cook on Full for 8 minutes, turning the dish twice. Allow to stand for 3 minutes. Using a fish slice, transfer the carp to a shallow dish. Cover and chill. Transfer the liquid into a jug and chill until lightly jellied. Spoon the jelly over the fish and serve.

Rollmops with Apricots

Serves 4

75 g/3 oz dried apricots
150 ml/¼ pt/2/3 cup cold water
3 bought rollmops with sliced onions
150 g/5 oz/2/3 cup crème fraîche
Mixed salad leaves
Crispbread

Wash the apricots and cut into bite-sized pieces. Place in a bowl with the cold water. Cover with an inverted plate and heat on Full for 5 minutes. Allow to stand for 5 minutes. Drain. Cut the rollmops into strips. Add to the apricots with the onions and crème fraîche. Mix well. Cover and leave to marinate in the refrigerator for 4–5 hours. Serve on salad leaves with crispbread.

Poached Kipper

Serves 1

Microwaving stops the smell permeating the house and leaves the kipper juicy and tender.

1 large undyed kipper, about 450 g/1 lb
120 ml/4 fl oz/½ cup cold water
Butter or margarine

Trim the kipper, discarding the tail. Soak for 3–4 hours in several changes of cold water to reduce saltiness, if wished, then drain. Place in a large, shallow dish with the water. Cover with clingfilm (plastic wrap) and slit it twice to allow steam to escape. Cook on Full for 4 minutes. Serve on a warmed plate with knob of butter or margarine.

Prawns Madras

Serves 4

25 g/1 oz/2 tbsp ghee or 15 ml/1 tbsp groundnut (peanut) oil
2 onions, chopped
2 garlic cloves, crushed
15 ml/1 tbsp hot curry powder
5 ml/1 tsp ground cumin
5 ml/1 tsp garam masala
Juice of 1 small lime
150 ml/¼ pt/2/3 cup fish or vegetable stock
30 ml/2 tbsp tomato purée (paste)
60 ml/4 tbsp sultanas (golden raisins)
450 g/1 lb/4 cups peeled prawns (shrimp), thawed if frozen
175 g/6 oz/¾ cup long-grain rice, boiled
Popadoms

Put the ghee or oil in a deep 20 cm/8 in diameter dish. Heat, uncovered, on Full for 1 minute. Thoroughly mix in the onions and garlic. Cook, uncovered, on Full for 3 minutes. Add the curry powder, cumin, garam masala and lime juice. Cook, uncovered, on Full for 3 minutes, stirring twice. Add the stock, tomato purée and sultanas. Cover with an inverted plate and cook on Full for 5 minutes. Drain the prawns if necessary, then add to the dish and stir round to combine. Cook, uncovered, on Full for 1½ minutes. Serve with the rice and popadoms.

Martini Plaice Rolls with Sauce

Serves 4

8 plaice fillets, 175 g/6 oz each, washed and dried
Salt and freshly ground black pepper
Juice of 1 lemon
2.5 ml/½ tsp Worcestershire sauce
25 g/1 oz/2 tbsp butter or margarine
4 shallots, peeled and chopped
100 g/3½ oz/1 cup cooked ham, cut into strips
400 g/14 oz mushrooms, thinly sliced
20 ml/4 tsp cornflour (cornstarch)
20 ml/4 tsp cold milk
250 ml/8 fl oz/1 cup chicken stock
150 g/¼ pt/2/3 cup single (light) cream
2.5 ml/½ tsp caster (superfine) sugar
1.5 ml/¼ tsp turmeric
10 ml/2 tsp martini bianco

Season the fish with salt and pepper. Marinate in the lemon juice and Worcestershire sauce for 15–20 minutes. Melt the butter or margarine in a saucepan (skillet). Add the shallots and fry (sauté) gently until soft and semi-transparent. Add the ham and mushrooms and stir-fry for 7 minutes. Blend the cornflour with the cold milk until smooth and add the remaining ingredients. Roll up the plaice fillets and spear with cocktail sticks (toothpicks). Arrange in a deep 20 cm/8 in diameter dish. Coat with the mushroom mixture. Cover with clingfilm (plastic wrap) and slit it twice to allow steam to escape. Cook on Full for 10 minutes.

Shellfish Ragout with Walnuts

Serves 4

30 ml/2 tbsp olive oil

1 onion, peeled and chopped

2 carrots, peeled and finely diced

3 celery stalks, cut into narrow strips

1 red (bell) pepper, seeded and cut into strips

1 green (bell) pepper, seeded and cut into strips

1 small courgette (zucchini), trimmed and thinly sliced

250 ml/8 fl oz/1 cup rosé wine

1 bouquet garni sachet

325 ml/11 fl oz/1 1/3 cups vegetable or fish stock

400 g/14 oz/1 large can chopped tomatoes

125 g/4 oz squid rings

125 g/4 oz cooked shelled mussels

200 g/7 oz lemon sole or flounder fillet, cut into chunks

4 giant prawns (jumbo shrimp), cooked

50 g/2 oz/½ cup walnuts, coarsely chopped

30 ml/2 tbsp stoned (pitted) black olives

10 ml/2 tsp gin

Juice of ½ small lemon

2.5 ml/½ tsp granulated sugar

1 baguette

30 ml/2 tbsp coarsely chopped basil leaves

Pour the oil into a 2.5 litre/4½ pt/11 cup dish. Heat, uncovered, on Full for 2 minutes. Add the prepared vegetables and toss in the oil to coat. Cover with clingfilm (plastic wrap) and slit it twice to allow steam to escape. Cook on Full for 5 minutes. Add the wine and bouquet garni. Cover as before and cook on Full for 5 minutes. Add the stock, tomatoes and fish. Re-cover and cook on Full for 10 minutes. Mix in all the remaining ingredients except the basil. Re-cover and cook on full for 4 minutes. Scatter with the basil and serve hot.

Cod Hot-pot

Serves 4

25 g/1 oz/2 tbsp butter or margarine
1 onion, peeled and chopped
2 carrots, peeled and finely diced
2 celery stalks, thinly sliced
150 ml/¼ pt/2/3 cup medium-dry white wine
400 g/14 oz skinned cod fillet, cut into large cubes
15 ml/1 tbsp cornflour (cornstarch)
75 ml/5 tbsp cold milk
350 ml/12 fl oz/1½ cups fish or vegetable stock
Salt and freshly ground black pepper
75 ml/5 tbsp chopped dill (dill weed)
300 ml/½ pt/1¼ cups double (heavy) cream, softly whipped
2 egg yolks

Place the butter or margarine in a 20 cm/8 in diameter casserole dish (Dutch oven). Heat, uncovered, on Full for 2 minutes. Mix in the vegetables and wine. Cover with clingfilm (plastic wrap) and slit it twice to allow steam to escape. Cook on Full for 5 minutes. Allow to stand for 3 minutes. Uncover. Add the fish to the vegetables. Mix the cornflour with the cold milk until smooth, then add to the casserole with the stock. Season. Cover as before and cook on Full for 8 minutes. Add the dill. Thoroughly mix the cream with the egg yolks and stir into the casserole. Cover and cook on Full for 1½ minutes.

Smoked Cod Hot-pot

Serves 4

Prepare as for Cod Hot-pot but substitute smoked cod fillet for fresh.

Monkfish in Golden Lemon Cream Sauce

Serves 6

300 ml/½ pt/1¼ cups full-cream milk
25 g/1 oz/2 tbsp butter or margarine, at kitchen temperature
675 g/1½ lb monkfish fillets, cut into bite-sized chunks
45 ml/3 tbsp plain (all-purpose) flour
2 large egg yolks
Juice of 1 large lemon
2.5–5 ml/½ –1 tsp salt
2.5 ml/½ tsp finely chopped tarragon
Cooked vol-au-vent cases (patty shells) or toasted ciabatta bread slices

Pour the milk into a jug and warm, uncovered, on Full for 2 minutes. Place the butter or margarine in a deep 20 cm/8 in diameter dish. Melt, uncovered, on Defrost for 1½ minutes. Coat the fish chunks in flour and add to the butter or margarine in the dish. Gently pour in the milk. Cover with clingfilm (plastic wrap) and slit it twice to allow steam to escape. Cook on Full for 7 minutes. Beat together the egg yolks, lemon juice and salt and stir into the fish. Cook, uncovered, on Full for 2 minutes. Allow to stand for 5 minutes. Stir round, sprinkle with the tarragon and serve in vol-au-vent cases or with slices of toasted ciabatta.

Sole in Golden Lemon Cream Sauce

Serves 6

Prepare as for Monkfish in Golden Lemon Cream Sauce, but substitute sole, cut into strips, for the monkfish chunks.

Salmon Hollandaise

Serves 4

4 salmon steaks, 175–200 g/6–7 oz each
150 ml/¼ pt water/2/3 cup water or dry white wine
2.5 ml/½ tsp salt
Hollandaise Sauce

Arrange the steaks round the sides of a deep 20 cm/8 in diameter dish. Add the water or wine. Sprinkle the fish with the salt. Cover with clingfilm (plastic wrap) and slit it twice to allow steam to escape. Cook on Defrost (to prevent the salmon spitting) for 16–18 minutes. Allow to stand for 4 minutes. Lift out on to four warmed plates with a fish slice, draining off the liquid. Coat each with the Hollandaise Sauce.

Salmon Hollandaise with Coriander

Serves 4

Prepare as for Salmon Hollandaise, but add 30 ml/2 tbsp chopped coriander (cilantro) to the sauce as soon as it has finished cooking. For additional flavour, mix in 10 ml/2 tsp chopped lemon balm.

Salmon Mayonnaise Flake

Serves 6

900 g/2 lb fresh salmon fillet, skinned
Salt and freshly ground black pepper
Melted butter or margarine (optional)
50 g/2 oz/½ cup flaked (slivered) almonds, toasted
1 small onion, finely chopped
30 ml/2 tbsp finely chopped parsley
5 ml/1 tsp chopped tarragon
200 ml/7 fl oz/scant 1 cup French-style mayonnaise
Lettuce leaves
Fennel sprays, to garnish

Divide the salmon into four portions. Arrange round the edge of a deep 25 cm/10 in diameter dish. Sprinkle with salt and pepper and trickle a little melted butter or margarine over the top if wished. Cover with clingfilm (plastic wrap) and slit it twice to allow steam to escape. Cook on Defrost for 20 minutes. Allow to cool to lukewarm, then flake the fish with two forks. Transfer to a bowl, add half the almonds and the onion, parsley and tarragon. Gently stir in the mayonnaise until well mixed and moist. Line a long serving dish with lettuce leaves. Arrange a line of salmon mayonnaise on top. Sprinkle with the remaining almonds and garnish with fennel.

Mediterranean-style Salmon Roast

Serves 6–8

1.5 kg/3lb portion middle-cut salmon
60 ml/4 tbsp olive oil
60 ml/4 tbsp lemon juice
60 ml/4 tbsp tomato purée (paste)
15 ml/1 tbsp chopped basil leaves
7.5 ml/1½ tsp salt
45 ml/3 tbsp small capers, drained
45 ml/3 tbsp chopped parsley

Wash the salmon, ensuring all scales are scraped off. Place in a deep 20 cm/8 in diameter dish. Whisk together the remaining ingredients and spoon over the fish. Cover with a plate and leave to marinate in the refrigerator for 3 hours. Cover with clingfilm (plastic wrap) and slit it twice to allow steam to escape. Cook on Full for 20 minutes, turning the dish twice. Divide into portions to serve.

Kedgeree with Curry

Serves 4

Once a breakfast dish, particularly associated with colonial days in India around the turn of the century, kedgeree is now more often served for lunch.

350 g/12 oz smoked haddock or cod fillet
60 ml/4 tbsp cold water
50 g/2 oz/¼ cup butter or margarine
225 g/8 oz/1 cup basmati rice
15 ml/1 tbsp mild curry powder
600 ml/1 pt/2½ cups boiling water
3 hard-boiled (hard-cooked) eggs
150 ml/¼ pt/2/3 cup single (light) cream
15 ml/1 tbsp chopped parsley
Salt and freshly ground black pepper
Parsley sprigs, to garnish

Put the fish into a shallow dish with the cold water. Cover with clingfilm (plastic wrap) and slit it twice to allow steam to escape. Cook on Full for 5 minutes. Drain. Flake up the flesh with two forks, removing the skin and bones. Place the butter or margarine in a round 1.75 litre/3 pt/7½ cup heatproof serving dish and melt on Defrost for 1½–2 minutes. Stir in the rice, curry powder and boiling water. Cover as before and cook on Full for 15 minutes. Chop two of the eggs and stir into the dish with the fish, cream and parsley, seasoning to taste.

Fork round, cover with an inverted plate and reheat on Full for 5 minutes. Slice the remaining egg. Remove the dish from the microwave and garnish with the sliced egg and parsley sprigs.

Kedgeree with Smoked Salmon

Serves 4

Prepare as for Kedgeree with Curry, but substitute 225 g/8 oz smoked salmon (lox), cut into strips, for the smoked haddock or cod. Smoked salmon does not need precooking.

Smoked Fish Quiche

Serves 6

175 g/6 oz shortcrust pastry (basic pie crust)
1 egg yolk, beaten
125 g/4 oz smoked fish such as mackerel, haddock, cod or trout, cooked and flaked
3 eggs
150 ml/¼ pt/2/3 cup soured (dairy sour) cream
30 ml/2 tbsp mayonnaise
Salt and freshly ground black pepper
75 g/3 oz/¾ cup Cheddar cheese, grated
Paprika
Mixed salad

Lightly butter a fluted 20 cm/8 in diameter glass or china flan dish. Roll out the pastry and use to line the greased dish. Prick well all over, especially where the side meets the base. Cook, uncovered, on Full for 6 minutes, turning the dish twice. If any bulges appear, press down with fingers protected by oven gloves. Brush the inside of the pastry case (pie shell) with the egg yolk. Cook on Full for 1 minute to seal any holes. Remove from the oven. Cover the base with the fish. Beat the eggs with the cream and mayonnaise, seasoning to taste. Pour into the quiche and sprinkle with the cheese and paprika. Cook, uncovered, on Full for 8 minutes. Serve warm with salad.

Louisiana Prawn Gumbo

Serves 8

3 onions, chopped

2 garlic cloves

3 celery stalks, finely chopped

1 green (bell) pepper, seeded and finely chopped

50 g/2 oz/¼ cup butter

60 ml/4 tbsp plain (all-purpose) flour

900 ml/1½ pt/3¾ cups hot vegetable or chicken stock

350 g/12 oz okra (ladies' fingers), topped and tailed

15 ml/1 tbsp salt

10 ml/2 tsp ground coriander (cilantro)

5 ml/1 tsp turmeric

2.5 ml/½ tsp ground allspice

30 ml/2 tbsp lemon juice

2 bay leaves

5–10 ml/1–2 tsp Tabasco sauce

450 g/1 lb/4 cups cooked peeled prawns (shrimp), thawed if frozen

350 g/12 oz/1½ cups long-grain rice, boiled

Place the onions in a 2.5 litre/4½ pt/11 cup bowl. Crush the garlic over the top. Add the celery and green pepper. Melt the butter on Full for 2 minutes. Stir in the flour. Cook, uncovered, on Full for 5–7 minutes, stirring four times and watching carefully in case of burning, until the mixture is a light biscuit-coloured roux. Gradually blend in the stock.

Set aside. Cut the okra into chunks and add to the vegetables with all the remaining ingredients except the Tabasco and prawns but including the roux mix. Cover with clingfilm (plastic wrap) and slit it twice to allow steam to escape. Cook on Full for 25 minutes. Allow to stand for 5 minutes. Stir in the Tabasco and prawns. Spoon into warmed deep bowls and add a mound of freshly cooked rice to each. Eat straight away.

Monkfish Gumbo

Serves 8

Prepare as for Louisiana Prawn Gumbo, but substitute the same weight of boned monkfish, cut into strips, for the prawns (shrimp). Cover with clingfilm (plastic wrap) and cook on Full for 4 minutes before transferring to serving bowls.

Mixed Fish Gumbo

Serves 8

Prepare as for Louisiana Prawn Gumbo, but substitute assorted cubed fish fillets for the prawns (shrimp).

Trout with Almonds

Serves 4

50 g/2 oz/¼ cup butter
15 ml/1 tbsp lemon juice
4 medium trout
50 g/2 oz/½ cup flaked (slivered) almonds, toasted
Salt and freshly ground black pepper
4 lemon wedges
Parsley sprigs

Melt the butter on Defrost for 1½ minutes. Stir in the lemon juice. Place the trout, head-to-tail, in a buttered 25 3 20 cm/10 3 8 in dish. Coat the fish with the butter mixture and sprinkle with the almonds and seasoning. Cover with clingfilm (plastic wrap) and slit it twice to allow steam to escape. Cook on Full for 9–12 minutes, turning the dish twice. Allow to stand for 5 minutes. Transfer to four warmed plates. Pour over the cooking liquid and garnish with the lemon wedges and parsley sprigs.

Prawns Provençale

Serves 4

225 g/8 oz/1 cup easy-cook long-grain rice
600 ml/1 pt/2½ cups hot fish or chicken stock
5 ml/1 tsp salt
15 ml/1 tbsp olive oil
1 onion, grated
1–2 garlic cloves, crushed
6 large very ripe tomatoes, blanched, skinned and chopped
15 ml/1 tbsp chopped basil leaves
5 ml/1 tsp dark soft brown sugar
450 g/1 lb/4 cups frozen peeled prawns (shrimp), unthawed
Salt and freshly ground black pepper
Chopped parsley

Place the rice in a 2 litre/3½ pt/8½ cup dish. Stir in the hot stock and salt. Cover with clingfilm (plastic wrap) and slit it twice to allow steam to escape. Cook on Full for 16 minutes. Allow to stand for 8 minutes for the rice to absorb all the moisture. Pour the oil into a 1.75 litre/3 pt/7½ cup serving dish. Heat, uncovered, on Full for 1½ minutes. Stir in the onion and garlic. Cook, uncovered, on Full for 3 minutes, stirring twice. Add the tomatoes with the basil and sugar. Cover with a plate and cook on Full for 5 minutes, stirring twice. Mix in the frozen prawns and seasoning to taste. Cover as before and cook on Full for 4 minutes, then gently separate the prawns. Re-cover and cook on Full for a further 3 minutes. Allow to stand. Cover the rice with a plate and reheat on Defrost for 5–6 minutes. Spoon on to four warmed plates and top with the fish and tomato mixture. Sprinkle with parsley and serve hot.

Plaice in Celery Sauce with Toasted Almonds

Serves 4

8 plaice fillets, total weight about 1 kg/2¼ lb
300 ml/10 fl oz/1 can condensed cream of celery soup
150 m/¼ pt/2/3 cup boiling water
15 ml/1 tbsp finely chopped parsley
30 ml/2 tbsp flaked (slivered) almonds, toasted

Roll up the fish fillets from head to tail, skin sides inside. Arrange round the edge of a deep 25 cm/10 in diameter buttered dish. Gently whisk together the soup and water and stir in the parsley. Spoon over the fish. Cover the dish with clingfilm (plastic wrap) and slit it twice to allow steam to escape. Cook on Full for 12 minutes, turning the dish twice. Allow to stand for 5 minutes. Cook on Full for a further 6 minutes. Spoon on to warmed plates and serve, sprinkled with the almonds.

Fillets in Tomato Sauce with Marjoram

Serves 4

Prepare as for Plaice in Celery Sauce with Toasted Almonds, but substitute condensed tomato soup for celery and 2.5 ml/½ tsp dried marjoram for the parsley.

Fillets in Mushroom Sauce with Watercress

Serves 4

Prepare as for Plaice in Celery Sauce with Toasted Almonds, but substitute condensed mushroom soup for celery and 30 ml/2 tbsp chopped watercress for the parsley.

Hashed Cod with Poached Eggs

Serves 4

This was found in a handwritten nineteenth-century notebook, belonging to the grandmother of an old friend.

675 g/1½ lb skinned cod fillet
10 ml/2 tsp melted butter or margarine or sunflower oil
Paprika
Salt and freshly ground black pepper
50 g/2 oz/¼ cup butter or margarine
8 large spring onions (scallions), trimmed and chopped
350 g/12 oz cold cooked potatoes, diced
150 ml/¼ pt/2/3 cup single (light) cream
5 ml/1 tsp salt
4 eggs
175 ml/6 fl oz/¾ cup hot water
5 ml/1 tsp vinegar

Arrange the fish in a shallow dish. Brush with some of the melted butter or margarine or oil. Season with paprika, salt and pepper. Cover with clingfilm (plastic wrap) and slit it twice to allow steam to escape. Cook on Defrost for 14–16 minutes. Flake up the fish with two forks, removing the bones. Put the remaining butter, margarine or oil into a 20 cm/8 in diameter casserole dish (Dutch oven). Heat, uncovered, on Defrost for 1½ –2 minutes. Mix in the onions. Cover with a plate and cook on Full for 5 minutes. Stir in the fish with the potatoes, cream and salt. Cover as before and reheat on Full for 5–7 minutes until very hot, stirring once or twice. Keep hot. To poach the eggs, gently break two into a small dish and add half the water and half the vinegar. Puncture the yolks with the tip of a knife. Cover with a plate and cook on Full for 2 minutes. Allow to stand for 1 minute. Repeat with the remaining eggs, hot water and vinegar. Spoon helpings of the hash on to four warmed plates and top each with an egg.

Haddock and Vegetables in Cider Sauce

Serves 4

50 g/2 oz/¼ cup butter or margarine
1 onion, thinly sliced and separated into rings
3 carrots, thinly sliced
50 g/2 oz button mushrooms, sliced
4 pieces filleted and skinned haddock or other white fish
5 ml/1 tsp salt
150 ml/¼ pt/2/3 cups medium-sweet cider
10 ml/2 tsp cornflour (cornstarch)
15 ml/1 tbsp cold water

Place half the butter or margarine in a deep 20 cm/8 in diameter dish. Melt, uncovered, on Defrost for about 1½ minutes. Add the onion, carrots and mushrooms. Arrange the fish on top. Sprinkle with the salt. Pour the cider gently over the fish. Dot with the remaining butter or margarine. Cover with clingfilm (plastic wrap) and slit it twice to allow steam to escape. Cook on Full for 8 minutes. In a glass jug, blend the cornflour smoothly with the cold water and gently strain in the fish liquor. Cook, uncovered, on Full for 2½ minutes until thickened, whisking every minute. Pour over the fish and vegetables. Spoon on to warmed plates and eat straight away.

Seaside Pie

Serves 4

For the topping:

700 g/1½ lb floury potatoes, unpeeled weight

75 ml/5 tbsp boiling water

15 ml/1 tbsp butter or margarine

75 ml/5 tbsp milk or single (light) cream

Salt and freshly ground pepper

Grated nutmeg

For the sauce:

300 ml/½ pt/1¼ cups cold milk

30 ml/2 tbsp butter or margarine

20 ml/4 tsp plain (all-purpose) flour

75 ml/5 tbsp Red Leicester or coloured Cheddar cheese, grated

5 ml/1 tsp wholegrain mustard

5 ml/1 tsp Worcestershire sauce

For the fish mixture:

450 g/1 lb skinned white fish fillet, at kitchen temperature

Melted butter or margarine

Paprika

60 ml/4 tbsp Red Leicester or coloured Cheddar cheese, grated

To make the topping, wash and peel the potatoes and cut into large cubes. Put in a 1.5 litre/2½ pt/6 cup dish with the boiling water. Cover with clingfilm (plastic wrap) and slit it twice to allow steam to escape. Cook on Full for 15 minutes, turning the dish twice. Allow to stand for 5 minutes. Drain and mash thoroughly with the butter or margarine and milk or cream, beating until fluffy. Season to taste with salt, pepper and nutmeg.

To make the sauce, heat the milk, uncovered, on Full for 1½ minutes. Set aside. Melt the butter or margarine, uncovered, on Defrost for 1–1½ minutes. Stir in the flour. Cook, uncovered, on Full for 30 seconds. Gradually blend in the milk. Cook on Full for about 4 minutes, beating every minute to ensure smoothness, until the sauce is thickened. Stir in the cheese with the remaining sauce ingredients.

To make the fish mixture, arrange the fillets in a shallow dish and brush with melted butter or margarine. Season with paprika, salt and pepper. Cover with clingfilm (plastic wrap) and slit it twice to allow steam to escape. Cook on Full for 5–6 minutes. Flake up the fish with two forks, removing any bones. Transfer to a buttered 1.75 litre/3 pt/7½ cup dish. Mix in the sauce. Cover with the potatoes and sprinkle with the cheese and extra paprika. Reheat, uncovered, on Full for 6–7 minutes.

Smoky Fish Toppers

Serves 2

2 frozen smoked haddock portions, 175 g/6 oz each
Freshly ground black pepper
1 small courgette (zucchini), sliced
1 small onion, thinly sliced
2 tomatoes, blanched, skinned and chopped
½ red (bell) pepper, seeded and cut into strips
15 ml/1 tbsp snipped chives

Arrange the fish in a deep 18 cm/7 in diameter dish. Season with pepper. Cover with clingfilm (plastic wrap) and slit it twice to allow steam to escape. Cook on Full for 8 minutes. Spoon the juices over the fish, then allow to stand for 1 minute. Place the vegetables in another medium-sized casserole dish (Dutch oven). Cover with a plate and cook on Full for 5 minutes, stirring once. Spoon the vegetables over the fish. Cover as before and cook on Full for 2 minutes. Sprinkle with the chives and serve.

Coley Fillets with Leek and Lemon Marmalade

Serves 2

An off-beat arrangement from Edinburgh's Sea Fish Authority, which also donated the next three recipes.

15 ml/1 tbsp butter
1 garlic clove, peeled and crushed
1 leek, slit and thinly sliced
2 coley fillets, 175 g/6 oz each, skinned
Juice of ½ lemon
10 ml/2 tsp lemon marmalade
Salt and freshly ground black pepper

Place the butter, garlic and leek in a deep 18 cm/7 in diameter dish. Cover with clingfilm (plastic wrap) and slit it twice to allow steam to escape. Cook on Full for 2½ minutes. Uncover. Arrange the fillets on top and sprinkle with half the lemon juice. Cover as before and cook on Full for 7 minutes. Transfer the fish to two warmed plates and keep hot. Mix the remaining lemon juice, the marmalade and seasoning into the fish juices and leek. Cover with a plate and cook on Full for 1½ minutes. Spoon over the fish and serve.

Seafish in a Jacket

Serves 4

4 baking potatoes, unpeeled but well scrubbed
450 g/1 lb white fish fillet, skinned and cubed
45 ml/3 tbsp butter or margarine
3 spring onions (scallions), trimmed and chopped
30 ml/2 tbsp wholegrain mustard
1.5 ml/¼ tsp paprika, plus extra for dusting
30–45 ml/2–3 tbsp plain yoghurt
Salt

Stand the potatoes directly on the turntable, cover with kitchen paper and cook on Full for 16 minutes. Wrap in a clean tea towel (dish cloth) and set aside. Place the fish in an 18 cm/7 in diameter casserole dish (Dutch oven) with the butter or margarine, spring onions, mustard and paprika. Cover with a plate and cook on Full for 7 minutes, stirring twice. Allow to stand for 2 minutes. Mix in the yoghurt and salt to taste. Cut a cross on top of each potato and squeeze gently to open out. Fill with the fish mixture, dust with paprika and eat hot.

Swedish Cod with Melted Butter and Egg

Serves 4

300 ml/½ pt/1¼ cups cold water
3 whole cloves
5 juniper berries
1 bay leaf, crumbled
2.5 ml/½ tsp mixed pickling spice
1 onion, quartered
10 ml/2 tsp salt
4 middle-cut fresh cod steaks, 225 g/8 oz each
75 g/3 oz/2/3 cup butter
2 hard-boiled (hard-cooked) eggs (pages 98–9), shelled and chopped

Put the water, cloves, juniper berries, bay leaf, pickling spice, onion quarters and salt in a glass jug. Cover with clingfilm (plastic wrap) and slit it twice to allow steam to escape. Cook on Full for 15 minutes. Strain. Place the fish in a deep 25 cm/10 in diameter dish and pour in the strained liquid. Cover with clingfilm and slit it twice to allow steam to escape. Cook on Full for 10 minutes, turning the dish twice. Transfer the fish to a warmed dish, using a fish slice, and keep hot. Melt the butter, uncovered, on Defrost for 2 minutes. Pour over the fish. Sprinkle with the chopped eggs and serve.

Seafood Stroganoff

Serves 4

30 ml/2 tbsp butter or margarine
1 garlic clove, crushed
1 onion, sliced
125 g/4 oz button mushrooms
700 g/1½ lb white fish fillet, skinned and cubed
150 ml/¼ pt/2/3 cup soured (dairy sour) cream or crème fraîche
Salt and freshly ground black pepper
30 ml/2 tbsp chopped parsley

Place the butter or margarine in a 20 cm/8 in diameter casserole dish (Dutch oven). Melt, uncovered, on Defrost for 2 minutes. Add the garlic, onion and mushrooms. Cover with clingfilm (plastic wrap) and slit it twice to allow steam to escape. Cook on Full for 3 minutes. Add the fish cubes. Cover as before and cook on Full for 8 minutes. Stir in the cream and season with salt and pepper. Cover again and cook on Full for 1½ minutes. Serve sprinkled with the parsley.

Fresh Tuna Stroganoff

Serves 4

Prepare as for Seafood Stroganoff, but substitute very fresh tuna for the white fish.

White Fish Ragout Supreme

Serves 4

30 ml/2 tbsp butter or margarine
1 onion, chopped
2 carrots, finely diced
6 celery stalks, thinly sliced
150 ml/¼ pt/2/3 cup white wine
400 g/14 oz skinned cod or haddock fillet, cubed
10 ml/2 tsp cornflour (cornstarch)
90 ml/6 tbsp single (light) cream
150 ml/¼ pt/2/3 cup vegetable stock
Salt and freshly ground black pepper
2.5 ml/½ tsp anchovy essence (extract) or Worcestershire sauce
30 ml/2 tbsp chopped dill (dill weed)
300 ml/½ pt/1¼ cups whipping cream
2 egg yolks

Place the butter or margarine in a 20 cm/8 in diameter casserole dish (Dutch oven). Heat, uncovered, on Full for 2 minutes. Add the vegetables and wine. Cover with clingfilm (plastic wrap) and slit it twice to allow steam to escape. Cook on Full for 5 minutes. Allow to stand for 3 minutes. Add the fish to the vegetables. Blend the cornflour smoothly with the cream, then mix in the stock. Season with salt, pepper and the anchovy essence or Worcestershire sauce. Pour over the fish. Cover as before and cook on Full for 8 minutes. Mix in the dill, then beat together the cream and egg yolks and stir into the fish mixture. Cover as before and cook on Defrost for 3 minutes.

Salmon Mousse

Serves 8

30 ml/2 tbsp powdered gelatine
150 ml/¼ pt/2/3 cup cold water
418 g/15 oz/1 large can red salmon
150 ml/¼ pt/2/3 cup creamy mayonnaise
15 ml/1 tbsp mild made mustard
10 ml/2 tsp Worcestershire sauce
30 ml/2 tbsp fruit chutney, chopped if necessary
Juice of ½ large lemon
2 large egg whites
A pinch of salt
Cress, cucumber slices, salad greens and slices of fresh lime, to garnish

Stir the gelatine into 75 ml/5 tbsp of the cold water and allow to stand for 5 minutes to soften. Melt, uncovered, on Defrost for 2½–3 minutes. Stir again and mix in the remaining water. Tip the contents of the can of salmon into a fairly large bowl and flake with a fork, removing any skin and bones, then mash fairly finely. Mix in the melted gelatine, the mayonnaise, mustard, Worcestershire sauce, chutney and lemon juice. Cover and chill until just beginning to thicken and set round the edges. Beat the egg whites to stiff peaks. Beat one-third into the setting salmon mixture with the salt. Fold in the remaining egg whites and transfer the mixture to a 1.5 litre/2½ pt/6 cup ring mould, first rinsed with cold water. Cover with clingfilm (plastic wrap) and chill for 8 hours until firm. Before serving, quickly dip the mould up to its rim in and out of cold water to loosen. Run a wet knife gently round the sides, then invert on to a large wetted serving dish. (The wetting stops the jelly sticking.) Garnish attractively with plenty of cress, cucumber slices, salad greens and lime slices.

Dieters' Salmon Mousse

Serves 8

Prepare as for Salmon Mousse, but substitute fromage frais or quark for the mayonnaise.

Crab Mornay

Serves 4

300 ml/½ pt/1¼ cups full-cream milk
10 ml/2 tsp mixed pickling spice
1 small onion, cut into 8 wedges
2 parsley sprigs
A pinch of nutmeg
30 ml/2 tbsp butter
30 ml/2 tbsp plain (all-purpose) flour
Salt and freshly ground black pepper
75 g/3 oz/¾ cup Gruyère (Swiss) cheese, grated
5 ml/1 tsp continental mustard
350 g/12 oz prepared light and dark crabmeat
Toast slices

Pour the milk into a glass or plastic jug and stir in the pickling spice, onion wedges, parsley and nutmeg. Cover with a plate and heat on Full for 5–6 minutes until the milk just begins to shiver. Strain. Put the butter into a 1.5 litre/2½ pt/6 cup bowl and melt on Defrost for 1½ minutes. Mix in the flour. Cook on Full for 30 seconds. Gradually blend in the warm milk. Cook on Full for about 4 minutes, whisking every minute, until the sauce comes to the boil and thickens. Season with salt and pepper and stir in the cheese and mustard. Cook on Full for 30 seconds or until the cheese melts. Stir in the crabmeat. Cover with a plate and reheat on Full for 2–3 minutes. Serve on freshly made toast.

Tuna Mornay

Serves 4

Prepare as for Crab Mornay, but substitute canned tuna in oil for the crabmeat. Flake up the flesh with two forks and add to the sauce with the oil from the can.

Red Salmon Mornay

Serves 4

Prepare as for Crab Mornay, but substitute canned red salmon, drained and flaked, for the crabmeat.

Seafood and Walnut Combo

Serves 4

45 ml/3 tbsp olive oil

1 onion, chopped

2 carrots, sliced

2 celery stalks, thinly sliced

1 red (bell) pepper, seeded and cut into strips

1 green (bell) pepper, seeded and cut into strips

1 small courgette (zucchini), thinly sliced

250 ml/8 fl oz/1 cup white wine

A pinch of mixed spice

300 ml/½ pt/1¼ cups fish or vegetable stock

450 g/1 lb ripe tomatoes, blanched, skinned and chopped

125 g/4 oz squid rings

400 g/14 oz plaice or lemon sole fillet, cut into squares

125 g/4 oz cooked mussels

4 large cooked prawns (shrimp)

50 g/2 oz/½ cup walnut halves or pieces

50 g/2 oz/1/3 cup sultanas (golden raisins)

A dash of sherry

Salt and freshly ground black pepper

Juice of 1 lemon

30 ml/2 tbsp chopped parsley

Heat the oil in a 2.5 litre/4½ pt/11 cup casserole dish (Dutch oven) on Full for 2 minutes. Add all the vegetables. Cook, uncovered, on Full for 5 minutes, stirring twice. Add the wine, spice, stock and tomatoes with all the fish and seafood. Cover with clingfilm (plastic wrap) and slit it twice to allow steam to escape. Cook on Full for 10 minutes. Stir in all the remaining ingredients except the parsley. Cover as before and cook on Full for 4 minutes. Uncover, sprinkle with the parsley and serve straight away.

Salmon Ring with Dill

Serves 8–10

125 g/4 oz/3½ slices loose-textured white bread
900 g/2 lb skinned fresh salmon fillet, cubed
10 ml/2 tsp bottled anchovy sauce
5–7.5 ml/1–1½ tsp salt
1 garlic clove, crushed
4 large eggs, beaten
25 g/1 oz fresh dill (dill weed)
White pepper

Lightly butter a deep 23 cm/9 in diameter dish. Crumb the bread in a food processor. Add all remaining ingredients. Pulse the machine until the mixture is just combined and the fish coarsely minced. Avoid over-mixing or the mixture will be heavy and dense. Spread smoothly into the prepared dish and push a baby jam (conserve) jar or straight-sided egg cup into the centre so that the mixture forms a ring. Cover with clingfilm (plastic wrap) and slit it twice to allow steam to escape. Cook on Full for 15 minutes, turning the dish twice. (The ring will shrink away from the side of the dish.) Allow to stand until cool, then re-cover and chill. Cut into wedges and serve. Leftovers can be used in sandwiches.

Mixed Fish Ring with Parsley

Serves 8–10

Prepare as for Salmon Ring with Dill, but substitute a mixture of skinned fresh salmon fillet, halibut and haddock for the salmon and 45 ml/3 tbsp chopped parsley for the dill.

Cod Casserole with Bacon and Tomatoes

Serves 6

30 ml/2 tbsp butter or margarine
225 g/8 oz gammon, coarsely chopped
2 onions, sliced
1 large green (bell) pepper, seeded and cut into strips
2 3 400 g/2 3 14 oz/2 large cans tomatoes
15 ml/1 tbsp mild continental mustard
45 ml/3 tbsp Cointreau or Grand Marnier
Salt and freshly ground black pepper
700 g/1½ lb skinned cod fillet, cubed
2 garlic cloves, crushed
60 ml/4 tbsp toasted brown breadcrumbs
15 ml/1 tbsp groundnut (peanut) or sunflower oil

Put the butter or margarine in a 2 litre/3½ pt/8½ cup casserole dish (Dutch oven). Heat, uncovered, on Full for 1½ minutes. Mix in the gammon, onions and pepper. Cook, uncovered, on Defrost for 10 minutes, stirring twice. Remove from the microwave. Work in the tomatoes, breaking them down with a fork, and stir in the mustard, liqueur and seasoning. Cover with clingfilm (plastic wrap) and slit it twice to allow steam to escape. Cook on Full for 6 minutes. Add the fish and garlic. Cover as before and cook on Medium for 10 minutes. Sprinkle with the breadcrumbs and trickle the oil over the top. Heat, uncovered, on Full for 1 minute.

Slimmers' Fish Pot

Serves 2

Tinged with a hottish jalapeno sauce and assertively spiced, enjoy this luxury fish feast with crusty French bread and rustic red wine.

2 onions, coarsely chopped

2 garlic cloves, crushed

15 ml/1 tbsp olive oil

400 g/14 oz/1 large can chopped tomatoes

200 ml/7 fl oz/scant 1 cup rosé wine

15 ml/1 tbsp Pernod or Ricard (pastis)

10 ml/2 tsp jalapeno sauce

2.5 ml/½ tsp hot pepper sauce

10 ml/2 tsp garam masala

1 bay leaf

2.5 ml/½ tsp dried oregano

2.5–5 ml/½–1 tsp salt

225 g/8 oz monkfish or skinned halibut, cut into strips

12 large cooked prawns (shrimp)

2 large scallops, cut into strips

30 ml/2 tbsp chopped coriander (cilantro), to garnish

Place the onions, garlic and oil in a 2 litre/3½ pt/8½ cup casserole dish (Dutch oven). Cover with a plate and cook on Full for 3 minutes. Mix in the remaining ingredients except the fish, shellfish and coriander. Cover as before and cook on Full for 6 minutes, stirring three times. Mix in the monkfish or halibut. Cover as before and cook on Defrost for 4 minutes until the fish whitens. Stir in the prawns and scallops. Cover as before and cook on Defrost for 1½ minutes. Stir round, ladle into deep plates and sprinkle each with coriander. Serve straight away.

Roast Chicken

Microwaved chicken can be succulent and attractively flavoured if it's treated with a suitable baste and left unstuffed.

1 oven-ready chicken, size as required

For the baste:
25 g/1 oz/2 tbsp butter or margarine
5 ml/1 tsp paprika
5 ml/1 tsp Worcestershire sauce
5 ml/1 tsp soy sauce
2.5 ml/½ tsp garlic salt or 5 ml/1 tsp garlic paste
5 ml/1 tsp tomato purée (paste)

Stand the washed and dried chicken in a dish big enough to hold it comfortably and also to fit the microwave. (It needn't be deep.) To make the baste, melt the butter or margarine on Full for 30–60 seconds. Stir in the remaining ingredients and spoon over the chicken. Cover with clingfilm (plastic wrap) and slit it twice to allow steam to escape. Cook on Full for 8 minutes per 450 g/1 lb, turning the dish every 5 minutes. Half-way through cooking, switch off the microwave and allow the bird to stand inside for 10 minutes, then complete the cooking. Allow to stand for a further 5 minutes. Transfer to a carving board, cover with foil and allow to stand for 5 minutes before carving.

Glazed Roast Chicken

Prepare as for Roast Chicken, but add 5 ml/1 tsp black treacle (molasses), 10 ml/2 tsp brown sugar, 5 ml/1 tsp lemon juice and 5 ml/1 tsp brown sauce to the baste. Allow an extra 30 seconds' cooking time.

Tex-Mex Chicken

Prepare as for Roast Chicken. After cooking, divide the bird into portions and put in a clean dish. Coat with bought salsa, medium to hot according to taste. Sprinkle with 225 g/8 oz/2 cups grated Cheddar cheese. Reheat, uncovered, on Defrost for about 4 minutes until the cheese melts and bubbles. Serve with canned refried beans and slices of avocado sprinkled with lemon juice.

Coronation Chicken

1 Roast Chicken

45 ml/3 tbsp white wine

30 ml/2 tbsp tomato purée (paste)

30 ml/2 tbsp mango chutney

30 ml/2 tbsp sieved (strained) apricot jam (conserve)

30 ml/2 tbsp water

Juice of ½ lemon

10 ml/2 tsp mild curry paste

10 ml/2 tsp sherry

300 ml/½ pt/1¼ cups thick mayonnaise

60 ml/4 tbsp whipped cream

225 g/8 oz/1 cup long-grain rice, boiled

Watercress

Follow the recipe for Roast Chicken, including the baste. After cooking, remove the meat from the bones and cut into bite-sized pieces. Put into a mixing bowl. Pour the wine into a dish and add the tomato purée, chutney, jam, water and lemon juice. Heat, uncovered, on Full for 1 minute. Allow to cool. Work in the curry paste, sherry and mayonnaise and fold in the cream. Combine with the chicken. Arrange a bed of rice on a large serving dish and spoon the chicken mixture over. Garnish with watercress.

Chicken Veronique

1 Roast Chicken
1 onion, finely grated
25 g/1 oz/2 tbsp butter or margarine
150 ml/¼ pt/2/3 cup crème fraîche
30 ml/2 tbsp white port or medium-dry sherry
60 ml/4 tbsp thick mayonnaise
10 ml/2 tsp made mustard
5 ml/1 tsp tomato ketchup (catsup)
1 small celery stalk, chopped
75 g/3 oz seedless green grapes
Small bunches of green or red seedless grapes, to garnish

Follow the recipe for Roast Chicken, including the baste. After cooking, remove the meat from the bones and cut into bite-sized pieces. Put into a mixing bowl. Put the onion in a small bowl with the butter or margarine and cook, uncovered, on Full for 2 minutes. In a third bowl, beat together the crème fraîche, port or sherry, mayonnaise, mustard, tomato ketchup and celery. Fold into the chicken with the cooked onion and the grapes. Spoon neatly into a serving dish and garnish with the bunches of grapes.

Chicken in Vinegar Sauce with Tarragon

Adapted from a recipe discovered in a top restaurant in Lyons, France, in the early seventies.

1 Roast Chicken
25 g/1 oz/2 tbsp butter or margarine
30 ml/2 tbsp cornflour (cornstarch)
15 ml/1 tbsp tomato purée (paste)
45 ml/3 tbsp double (heavy) cream
45 ml/3 tbsp malt vinegar
Salt and freshly ground black pepper

Follow the recipe for Roast Chicken, including the baste. Cut the cooked bird into six portions, cover with foil and keep hot on a plate. To make the sauce, pour the chicken cooking juices into a measuring jug and make up to 250 ml/8 fl oz/1 cup with hot water. Put the butter or margarine in a separate dish and heat, uncovered, on Full for 1 minute. Stir in the cornflour, tomato purée, cream and vinegar, and season to taste with salt and freshly ground black pepper. Gradually blend in the hot chicken juices. Cook, uncovered, on Full for 4–5 minutes until thickened and bubbly, whisking every minute. Pour over the chicken and serve straight away.

Danish Roast Chicken with Parsley Stuffing

Prepare as for Roast Chicken, but make several slits in the uncooked chicken skin and pack with small parsley sprigs. Put 25 g/1 oz/2 tbsp garlic butter in the body cavity. Then proceed as in the recipe.

Chicken Simla

An Anglo-Indian speciality belonging to the days of the Raj.

1 Roast Chicken
15 ml/1 tbsp butter
5 ml/1 tsp finely chopped root ginger
5 ml/1 tsp garlic purée (paste)
2.5 ml/½ tsp turmeric
2.5 ml/½ tsp paprika
5 ml/1 tsp salt
300 ml/½ pt/1¼ cups whipping cream
Fried (sautéed) onion rings, home-made or bought, to garnish

Follow the recipe for Roast Chicken, including the baste. After cooking, divide the bird into six pieces and keep hot on a large plate or in a dish. Heat the butter in a 600 ml/1 pt/2½ cup dish on Full for 1 minute. Add the ginger and garlic purée. Cook, uncovered, on Full for 1½ minutes. Mix in the turmeric, paprika and salt, then the cream. Heat, uncovered, on Full for 4–5 minutes until the cream begins to bubble, whisking at least four times. Pour over the chicken and garnish with onion rings.

Spicy Chicken with Coconut and Coriander

Serves 4

A delicately spiced curry dish from southern Africa.

8 chicken portions, 1.25 kg/2¾ lb in all

45 ml/3 tbsp desiccated (shredded) coconut

1 green chilli, about 8 cm/3 in long, seeded and chopped

1 garlic clove, crushed

2 onions, grated

5 ml/1 tsp turmeric

5 ml/1 tsp ground ginger

10 ml/2 tsp mild curry powder

90 ml/6 tbsp coarsely chopped coriander (cilantro)

150 ml/¼ pt/2/3 cup canned coconut milk

125 g/4 oz/½ cup cottage cheese with chives

Salt

175 g/6 oz/¾ cup long-grain rice, boiled

Chutney, to serve

Skin the chicken. Arrange round the edge of a deep 25 cm/10 in diameter dish, pushing the pieces closely together so they fit snugly. Cover with clingfilm (plastic wrap) and slit it twice to allow steam to escape. Cook on Full for 10 minutes, turning the dish twice. Place the coconut in a bowl with all the remaining ingredients except the rice. Stir well. Uncover the chicken and coat with the coconut mixture. Cover as before and cook on Full for 10 minutes, turning the dish four times. Serve in deep plates on a mound of rice with chutney handed separately.

Spicy Rabbit

Serves 4

Prepare as for Spicy Chicken with Coconut and Coriander, but substitute eight rabbit portions for the chicken.

Spicy Turkey

Serves 4

Prepare as for Spicy Chicken with Coconut and Coriander, but substitute eight 175 g/6 oz pieces of boned turkey breast fillet for the chicken.

Chicken Bredie with Tomatoes

Serves 6

A South African stew, using the people's most popular combination of ingredients.

30 ml/2 tbsp sunflower or corn oil
3 onions, finely chopped
1 garlic clove, finely chopped
1 small green chilli, seeded and chopped
4 tomatoes, blanched, skinned and sliced
750 g/1½ lb boned chicken breasts, cut into small cubes
5 ml/1 tsp dark soft brown sugar
10 ml/2 tsp tomato purée (paste)
7.5–10 ml/1½ –2 tsp salt

Pour the oil into a deep 25 cm/10 in diameter dish. Add the onions, garlic and chilli and mix in thoroughly. Cook, uncovered, for 5 minutes. Add the remaining ingredients to the dish and make a small hollow in the centre with an egg cup so the mixture forms a ring. Cover with clingfilm (plastic wrap) and slit it twice to allow steam to escape. Cook on Full for 14 minutes, turning the dish four times. Allow to stand for 5 minutes before serving.

Chinese Red Cooked Chicken

Serves 4

A sophisticated Chinese stew, the chicken taking on a mahogany colour as it simmers in the sauce. Eat with plenty of boiled rice to absorb the salty juices.

6 Chinese dried mushrooms
8 large chicken drumsticks, 1 kg/2¼ lb in all
1 large onion, grated
60 ml/4 tbsp finely chopped preserved ginger
75 ml/5 tbsp sweet sherry
15 ml/1 tbsp black treacle (molasses)
Grated peel from 1 tangerine or similar loose-skinned citrus fruit
50 ml/2 fl oz/3½ cup soy sauce

Soak the mushrooms in hot water for 30 minutes. Drain and cut into strips. Slash the fleshy parts of the drumsticks and arrange round the edge of a deep 25 cm/10 in diameter dish with the bony ends pointing towards the centre. Cover with clingfilm (plastic wrap) and slit it twice to allow steam to escape. Cook on Full for 12 minutes, turning the dish three times. Mix together the remaining ingredients, including the mushrooms, and spoon over the chicken. Cover as before and cook on Full for 14 minutes. Allow to stand for 5 minutes before serving.

Aristocratic Chicken Wings

Serves 4

A centuries-old Chinese recipe, favoured by the élite and eaten with egg noodles.

8 Chinese dried mushrooms
6 spring onions (scallions), coarsely chopped
15 ml/1 tbsp groundnut (peanut) oil
900 g/2 lb chicken wings
225 g/8 oz canned sliced bamboo shoots
30 ml/2 tbsp cornflour (cornstarch)
45 ml/3 tbsp Chinese rice wine or medium-dry sherry
60 ml/4 tbsp soy sauce
10 ml/2 tsp finely chopped fresh root ginger

Soak the mushrooms in hot water for 30 minutes. Drain and cut into quarters. Put the onions and oil in a deep 25 cm/10 in diameter dish. Cook, uncovered, on Full for 3 minutes. Stir round. Arrange the chicken wings in the dish, leaving a small hollow in the centre. Cover with clingfilm (plastic wrap) and slit it twice to allow steam to escape. Cook on Full for 12 minutes, turning the dish three times. Uncover. Coat with the bamboo shoots and the liquid from the can and scatter the mushrooms over the top. Blend the cornflour smoothly with the rice wine or sherry. Add the remaining ingredients. Spoon over the chicken and vegetables. Cover as before and cook on Full for 10–12 minutes until the liquid is bubbling. Allow to stand for 5 minutes before serving.

Chicken Chow Mein

Serves 4

½ *cucumber, peeled and cubed*
275 g/10 oz/2½ *cups cold cooked chicken, cut into small cubes*
450 g/1 lb *fresh mixed vegetables for stir-frying*
30 ml/2 tbsp *soy sauce*
30 ml/2 tbsp *medium-dry sherry*
5 ml/1 tsp *sesame oil*
2.5 ml/½ tsp *salt*
Boiled Chinese noodles, to serve

Place the cucumber and chicken in a 1.75 litre/3 pt/7½ cup dish. Mix in all the remaining ingredients. Cover with a large plate and cook on Full for 10 minutes. Allow to stand for 3 minutes before serving with Chinese noodles.

Chicken Chop Suey

Serves 4

Prepare as for Chicken Chow Mein, but substitute boiled long-grain rice for the noodles.

Express Marinaded Chinese Chicken

Serves 3

Authentic tasting but fast as can be. Eat with rice or noodles and Chinese pickles.

6 chunky chicken thighs, about 750 g/1½ lb in all
125 g/4 oz/1 cup sweetcorn kernels, half thawed if frozen
1 leek, chopped
60 ml/4 tbsp bought Chinese marinade

Place the chicken in a deep bowl and add the remaining ingredients. Mix well. Cover and chill for 4 hours. Stir. Transfer to a deep 23 cm/9 in diameter dish, arranging the chicken round the edge. Cover with clingfilm (plastic wrap) and slit it twice to allow steam to escape. Cook on Full for 16 minutes, turning the dish four times. Allow to stand for 5 minutes before serving.

Hong Kong Chicken with Mixed Vegetables and Bean Sprouts

Serves 2–3

4 Chinese dried mushrooms
1 large onion, chopped
1 carrot, grated
15 ml/1 tbsp groundnut (peanut) oil
2 garlic cloves, crushed
225 g/8 oz/2 cups cooked chicken, cut into strips
275 g/10 oz bean sprouts
15 ml/1 tbsp soy sauce
1.5 ml/¼ tsp sesame oil
A good pinch of cayenne pepper
2.5 ml/½ tsp salt
Boiled rice or Chinese noodles, to serve

Soak the mushrooms in hot water for 30 minutes. Drain and cut into strips. Place the onion, carrot and oil in a 1.75 litre/3 pt/7½ cup dish. Cook, uncovered, on Full for 3 minutes. Stir in the remaining ingredients. Cover with clingfilm (plastic wrap) and slit it twice to allow steam to escape. Cook on Full for 5 minutes, turning the dish three times. Allow to stand for 5 minutes before serving with rice or noodles.

Chicken with Golden Dragon Sauce

Serves 4

4 large fleshy chicken joints, 225 g/8 oz each, skinned
Plain (all-purpose) flour
1 small onion, chopped
2 garlic cloves, crushed
30 ml/2 tbsp soy sauce
30 ml/2 tbsp medium-dry sherry
30 ml/2 tbsp groundnut (peanut) oil
60 ml/4 tbsp lemon juice
60 ml/4 tbsp light soft brown sugar
45 ml/3 tbsp melted and sieved (strained) apricot jam (conserve)
5 ml/1 tsp ground coriander (cilantro)
3–4 drops hot pepper sauce
Bean sprout salad and Chinese noodles, to serve

Slash the thick parts of the chicken joints in several places with a sharp knife, dust with flour, then arrange in a deep 25 cm/10 in diameter dish. Thoroughly stir together the remaining ingredients. Pour over the chicken. Cover the dish loosely with kitchen paper and leave to marinate in the refrigerator for 4–5 hours, turning the joints over twice. Arrange the slashed sides uppermost, then cover the dish with clingfilm (plastic wrap) and slit it twice to allow steam to escape. Cook on Full for 22 minutes, turning the dish four times. Serve on a bed of noodles and coat with juices from dish.

Ginger Chicken Wings with Lettuce

Serves 4–5

1 large cos (romaine) lettuce, shredded

2.5 cm/1 in piece root ginger, thinly sliced

2 garlic cloves, crushed

15 ml/1 tbsp groundnut (peanut) oil

300 ml/½ pt/1¼ cups boiling chicken stock

30 ml/2 tbsp cornflour (cornstarch)

2.5 ml/½ tsp five spice powder

60 ml/4 tbsp cold water

5 ml/1 tsp soy sauce

5 ml/1 tsp salt

1 kg/2¼ lb chicken wings

Boiled rice or Chinese noodles, to serve

Put the lettuce, ginger, garlic and oil into a fairly large casserole dish (Dutch oven). Cover with a plate and cook on Full for 5 minutes. Uncover and add the boiling stock. Blend the cornflour and five spice powder smoothly with the cold water. Stir in the soy sauce and salt. Mix into the lettuce mixture with the chicken wings, tossing gently until thoroughly combined. Cover with clingfilm (plastic wrap) and slit it twice to allow steam to escape. Cook on Full for 20 minutes, turning the dish four times. Allow to stand for 5 minutes before serving with rice or noodles.

Bangkok Coconut Chicken

Serves 4

The genuine article, made in my kitchen by a young Thai friend.

4 part-boned chicken breasts, 175 g/6 oz each
200 ml/7 fl oz/scant 1 cup creamed coconut
Juice of 1 lime
30 ml/2 tbsp cold water
2 garlic cloves, crushed
5 ml/1 tsp salt
1 stalk lemon grass, halved lengthways, or 6 lemon balm leaves
2–6 green chillies or 1.5–2.5 ml/¼–½ tsp dried red chilli powder
4–5 fresh lime leaves
20 ml/4 tsp chopped coriander (cilantro)
175 g/6 oz/¾ cup long-grain rice, boiled

Arrange the chicken round the edge of a deep 20 cm/8 in diameter dish, leaving a hollow in the centre. Cover with clingfilm (plastic wrap) and slit it twice to allow steam to escape. Cook on Full for 6 minutes, turning the dish twice. Combine the coconut cream, lime juice and water, then stir in the garlic and salt and pour over the chicken. Sprinkle on the lemon grass or lemon balm leaves, chillies to taste and lime leaves. Cover as before and cook on Full for 8 minutes, turning the dish three times. Allow to stand for 5 minutes. Uncover and stir in the coriander, then serve with the rice.

Chicken Satay

Serves 8 as a starter, 4 as a main course

For the marinade:

30 ml/2 tbsp groundnut (peanut) oil

30 ml/2 tbsp soy sauce

1 garlic clove, crushed

900 g/2 lb boned chicken breast, cubed

For the satay sauce:

10 ml/2 tsp groundnut oil

1 onion, chopped

2 green chillies, each about 8 cm/3 in long, seeded and finely chopped

2 garlic cloves, crushed

150 ml/¼ pt/2/3 cup boiling water

60 ml/4 tbsp crunchy peanut butter

10 ml/2 tsp wine vinegar

2.5 ml/½ tsp salt

175 g/6 oz/¾ cup long-grain rice, boiled (optional)

To make the marinade, combine the oil, soy sauce and garlic in a mixing bowl and add the chicken, stirring well to coat thoroughly. Cover and chill for 4 hours in winter, 8 in summer.

To make the sauce, pour the oil into a medium-sized dish or bowl and add the onion, chillies and garlic. Before completing the sauce, thread the chicken cubes on eight oiled skewers. Arrange, four at a time, on a large plate like the spokes of a wheel. Cook, uncovered, on Full for 5 minutes, turning over once. Repeat with the remaining four skewers. Keep hot. To finish the sauce, cover the bowl with clingfilm (plastic wrap) and slit it twice to allow steam to escape. Cook on Full for 2 minutes. Stir in the boiling water, peanut butter, vinegar and salt. Cook, uncovered, for 3 minutes, stirring once. Allow to stand for 30 seconds and serve, with the rice if a main course.

Peanut Chicken

Serves 4

4 boned chicken breasts, 175 g/6 oz each
125 g/4 oz/½ cup smooth peanut butter
2.5 ml/½ tsp ground ginger
2.5 ml/½ tsp garlic salt
10 ml/2 tsp mild curry powder
Chinese hoisin sauce
Boiled Chinese noodles, to serve

Arrange the chicken round the edge of a deep 23 cm/9 in diameter dish, leaving a hollow in the centre. Put the peanut butter, ginger, garlic salt and curry powder in a small dish and heat, uncovered, on Full for 1 minute. Spread evenly over the chicken, then coat lightly with hoisin sauce. Cover with clingfilm (plastic wrap) and slit it twice to allow steam to escape. Cook on Full for 16 minutes, turning the dish four times. Allow to stand for 5 minutes before serving with Chinese noodles.

Indian Chicken with Yoghurt

Serves 4

A fuss-free curry, fast to put together. It is low in fat so recommended for slimmers, perhaps with a side dish of cauliflower and a slice or two of seedy bread.

750 g/1½ lb skinned chicken thighs
150 ml/¼ pt/2/3 cup plain yoghurt
15 ml/1 tbsp milk
5 ml/1 tsp garam masala
1.5 ml/¼ tsp turmeric
5 ml/1 tsp ground ginger
5 ml/1 tsp ground coriander (cilantro)
5 ml/1 tsp ground cumin
15 ml/1 tbsp corn or sunflower oil
45 ml/3 tbsp hot water
60 ml/4 tbsp coarsely chopped coriander, to garnish

Place the chicken in a deep 30 cm/12 in diameter dish. Beat together all the remaining ingredients and spoon over the chicken. Cover and marinate in the refrigerator for 6–8 hours. Cover with a plate and warm through on Full for 5 minutes. Stir the chicken round. Cover the dish with clingfilm (plastic wrap) and slit it twice to allow steam to escape. Cook on Full for 15 minutes, turning the dish four times. Allow to stand for 5 minutes. Uncover and sprinkle with the chopped coriander before serving.

Japanese Chicken with Eggs

Serves 4

100 ml/3½ fl oz/6½ tbsp hot chicken or beef stock
60 ml/4 tbsp medium-dry sherry
30 ml/2 tbsp teriyaki sauce
15 ml/1 tbsp light soft brown sugar
250 g/9 oz/1¼ cups cooked chicken, cut into strips
4 large eggs, beaten
175 g/6 oz/¾ cup long-grain rice, boiled

Pour the stock, sherry and teriyaki sauce into a shallow 18 cm/7 in diameter dish. Stir in the sugar. Cover with clingfilm (plastic wrap) and slit it twice to allow steam to escape. Cook on Full for 5 minutes. Uncover and stir round. Mix in the chicken and pour the eggs over the top. Cook, uncovered, on Full for 6 minutes, turning the dish three times. To serve, spoon the rice into four warmed bowls and top with the chicken and egg mixture.

Portuguese Chicken Casserole

Serves 4

25 g/1 oz/2 tbsp butter or margarine or 25 ml/1½ tbsp olive oil
2 onions, quartered
2 garlic cloves, crushed
4 chicken joints, 900 g/2 lb in all
125 g/4 oz/1 cup cooked gammon, cut into small cubes
3 tomatoes, blanched, skinned and chopped
150 ml/¼ pt/2/3 cup dry white wine
10 ml/2 tsp French mustard
7.5–10 ml/1½–2 tsp salt

Put the butter, margarine or oil into a 20 cm/8 in diameter casserole dish (Dutch oven). Heat, uncovered, on Full for 1 minute. Stir in the onions and garlic. Cook, uncovered, on Full for 3 minutes. Add the chicken. Cover with clingfilm (plastic wrap) and slit it twice to allow steam to escape. Cook on Full for 14 minutes, turning the dish twice. Mix in the remaining ingredients. Cover as before and cook on Full for 6 minutes. Allow to stand for 5 minutes before serving.

English-style Spicy Chicken Casserole

Serves 4

Prepare as for Portuguese Chicken Casserole, but substitute medium-dry cider for the wine and add 5 quartered pickled walnuts with the other ingredients. Allow an extra 1 minute cooking time.

Compromise Tandoori Chicken

Serves 8 as a starter, 4 as a main course

An Indian dish traditionally made in a clay oven or tandoor, but this microwave version is entirely acceptable.

8 chicken pieces, about 1.25 kg/2¾ lb in all
250 ml/8 fl oz/1 cup thick Greek-style plain yoghurt
30 ml/2 tbsp tandoori spice mix
10 ml/2 tsp ground coriander (cilantro)
5 ml/1 tsp paprika
5 ml/1 tsp turmeric
30 ml/2 tbsp lemon juice
2 garlic cloves, crushed
7.5 ml/1½ tsp salt
Indian bread and mixed salad, to serve

Slash the fleshy parts of the chicken in several places. Lightly whip the yoghurt with all the remaining ingredients. Arrange the chicken in a deep 25 cm/10 in diameter dish and coat with the tandoori mix. Cover loosely with kitchen paper and marinate for 6 hours in the refrigerator.

Turn over, baste with the marinade and chill for a further 3–4 hours, covered as before. Cover with clingfilm (plastic wrap) and slit it twice to allow steam to escape. Cook on Full for 20 minutes, turning the dish four times. Uncover the dish and turn the chicken. Cover again with clingfilm and cook on Full for a further 7 minutes. Allow to stand for 5 minutes before serving.